Creative
Juice

network

Creative
Juice

45 Re-Crafting Projects to
Make with Recycled Stuff

**Cathie Filian &
Steve Piacenza**

LARK BOOKS

A Division of Sterling Publishing Co., Inc.
New York

Series Editor: Dawn Cusick

Series Designer: Thom Gaines

Cover Designer: DIY Network, Stewart Pack

Page Designer: Matt Paden

Contributing Writer: Susan Brill

Production: Jackie Kerr

Photography: Zuzanna Pakula Vel Rutka

10 9 8 7 6 5 4 3 2 1

First Edition

Published by Lark Books, A Division of
Sterling Publishing Co., Inc.
387 Park Avenue South, New York, N.Y. 10016

Distributed in Canada by Sterling Publishing,
c/o Canadian Manda Group, 165 Dufferin Street
Toronto, Ontario, Canada M6K 3H6

Distributed in the United Kingdom by GMC Distribution Services,
Castle Place, 166 High Street, Lewes, East Sussex, England BN7 1XU

Distributed in Australia by Capricorn Link (Australia) Pty Ltd.,
P.O. Box 704, Windsor, NSW 2756 Australia

If you have questions or comments about this book, please contact:
Lark Books
67 Broadway
Asheville, NC 28801
(828) 253-0467

Manufactured in China

ISBN 13: 978-1-60059-148-8
ISBN 10: 1-60059-148-5

Creative Juice **Contents**

Creative Juice

Welcome to *Creative Juice!*

This book celebrates a craft niche known as Re-Crafting. Simply, Re-Crafting is the process of transforming old materials into something new. The finished projects are hip and creative, and the process employs a spirit of inventiveness and imagination that's both fun and exhilarating.

The book is divided into five chapters, each filled with a fun range of great projects to make. The first chapter, Adorn, features wearable projects. Learn how to craft a clever purse from a beach towel or a pair of old jeans, or make jewelry from buttons, beads, and game pieces. The second chapter, Decorate, contains creative lighting projects made from everyday materials. The third chapter, Give, focuses on easy-to-make presents such as bracelets, scented pomanders, tea soaps, and more, plus simple gift card and wrapping projects for the perfect gift presentation.

The fourth chapter, Play, includes projects that celebrate young imaginations. You'll find puppets, party hats, travel games, and more. And the final chapter, Remember, presents a creative selection of memory projects perfect for showcasing special photographs of family and friends.

Our DIY Network show, *Creative Juice,* features a range of projects that are well suited to both novice and advanced crafters. As we do on the show, we've chosen projects for this book that are easy and affordable to make. You probably have many of the materials and tools you need already, and those you don't have are easily found at local craft and hardware stores.

Feel free to customize the projects to reflect your own taste and style, or go in a completely new direction. We hope this book will be a source of inspiration to get your own creative juices flowing!

Cathie Filian

Steve Piacenza

Cathie Filian & Steve Piacenza
Co-hosts of DIY Network's *Creative Juice*

Creative Juice

diy network

1

Adorn

Got an old pair of jeans that don't fit anymore? Don't toss them, throw them over your shoulder in a fun pants purse. Re-craft an out-of-date item into a stylish fashion accessory. Everything from belts and bleached Tees to handbags and baubles. This chapter is full of tons of creative ideas to dress up your wardrobe with accessories that will have you feeling like a true fashion diva.

Cathie   Steve

TOWEL BEACH BAG

Off to the beach? Don't forget your towel—your towel tote bag, that is. Old hand towels can be easily transformed into the perfect beach bag with just a few stitches. Wet swimsuit? No worries. This bag is the perfect accessory for a day in the sun—or the water.

You Will Need

2 hand towels, different colors

Scissors

Coordinating ribbon (narrower width than the woven band on each end of the towel)

Sewing pins

Sewing machine

Hand-sewing needle

Heavy-duty thread or embroidery floss

2 acrylic purse handles

In this project, you'll sew two hand towels together, trim them with ribbon, and attach pre-made purse handles for a great bag for the beach!

1 Lay the towels on top of each other and trim them so they are straight and the same size (photo A). One towel will be the outer bag and the other will be the lining of the bag.

2 Working on the outer towel, pin the decorative ribbon across the existing band on both edges of the towel (photo B). Sew it in place.

A

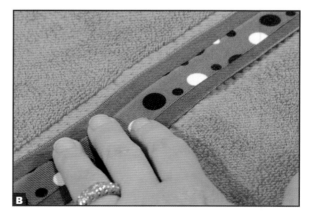

B

3 Lay the two towels on your work surface, right sides together, and pin around all sides (photo C). Sew all sides with a ⅝-inch seam allowance, leaving a 6-inch opening at the center of one of the long sides of the bag for turning the fabric out later.

4 Trim the seams at the corners and along the sides to remove any excess bulk, then turn the bag right side out. Hand-stitch the opening shut using heavy-duty thread.

5 Fold the sewn piece in half with the right side of the bag out and the ribbon ends toward the top. Create the side seams by top stitching down the sides with a 1-inch seam allowance (photo D). This will be very thick fabric—sewing through four layers—so set your machine accordingly with a long stitch length and lighter pressure on the presser foot.

CREATING SMOOTH FLAT SEAMS

For flat seams that don't add extra bulk to the edges of your bag, trim the seam before turning the bag right side out. Trim corners by cutting a 45-degree angle across the corner of the material, ⅛ to ¼ inch from the stitched corner. (Be careful—if you cut too close to the seam, the corner may not hold up with use.) For the side seams, layer the seam allowances by cutting one layer to about one-third of the allowance and the other to about two-thirds of the allowance. This layering will allow the thick fabric of the towels to lay flatter in the bag and not add a bulky ridge.

6 Using heavy-duty thread or embroidery floss, sew the handles to the inside of the opening of the bag, as closely to the top as possible (photo E).

E

TIPS | DIY Network Crafts

BUYING PURSE HANDLES

Fabric shcps and craft stores carry a wide variety of purse handles—everything from bamboo to acrylic. Or, instead of buying new purse handles, salvage some from old worn-out purses or off a vintage bag.

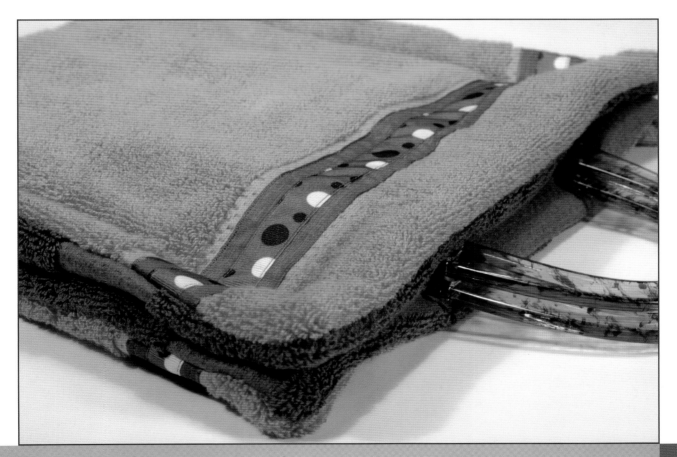

GAME-PIECE CHARMS

You've got game with these playful necklace charms. Bits of this and bits of that are recycled into fun and fashionable charms perfect for game night. String just one on a chain or use an assortment. Play with the possibilities.

▰ **PROJECT SUMMARY** ▰

A simple beavertail pendant backing turns your favorite game piece into wearable fun in this project. Just glue on the backing, cover with felt, add a jump ring, and string onto a chain.

You Will Need

Game piece	Craft glue
Metal glue	Round-nosed pliers
Beavertail pendant backing	Jump ring
Scrap felt	Old necklace chain

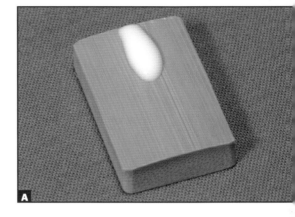

1 Apply metal glue to the back of the game piece. Place the pendant backing on the glue, making sure the loop on the backing hangs over the top edge of the game piece (photo A). Allow the glue to dry.

2 Cut a scrap of felt slightly smaller than the game piece and glue it to the back of the game piece, over the pendant backing, using craft glue (photo B).

3 Use round-nosed pliers to attach a jump ring through the pendant hole (photo C), and attach it to the necklace chain.

TIPS | DIY Network Crafts

PLAY FAIR

These charms are so hot you'll be tempted to slip your favorite letter from the family word game thinking no one will notice. (They will!) Instead, hunt out used games at thrift or secondhand stores. Pick a cool classic game, or find an obscure one that will make your charm a real conversation piece.

BOTTLE-CAP CHARMS

Cap off your accessories with a custom-designed, bottle-top charm that is sure to get the looks! Combine it with other charms on your necklace for color and dimension, or wear it alone.

Make tons of bottle-cap charms to mix and match with your outfits. Just use decorative scrap paper inside the cap and a beavertail pendant backing outside. Add a jump ring and wear on your favorite necklace or bracelet.

You Will Need

- 1" circle punch
- Decorative paper scrap
- Tacky glue
- Bottle cap
- Dimensional adhesive, clear
- Sewing pin
- Beavertail pendant backing
- Scrap felt
- Craft glue
- Metal glue
- Beavertail pendant backing
- Scrap felt
- Craft glue
- Round-nosed pliers
- Jump ring
- Old necklace chain or strap

1 Use the 1-inch circle punch to cut the decorative paper scrap.

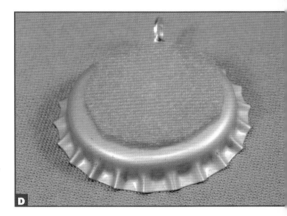

2 Using tacky glue, glue the paper (face up) to the inside of the bottle cap (photo A) and allow it to dry.

3 Seal the image with a thick coating of the dimensional adhesive and allow to dry following the manufacturer's instructions. Try not to move the bottle cap while it is drying. If an air bubble appears, pop it with a pin (photo B).

4 Hold the bottle cap so the design is upright, as you will wear it on the chain. Turn the cap over and apply metal glue to the back. Place the pendant backing in the glue, making sure the loop on the backing extends over the top edge of the cap (photo C). Allow the glue to dry.

5 Cut a scrap of felt slightly smaller than the flat surface of the bottle cap, and glue it to the back of the cap, covering the pendant backing (photo D).

6 Use round-nosed pliers to attach a jump ring through the hole on the pendant and attach to your necklace (photo E).

TIPS | DIY Network Crafts

CUTTING UP

Don't have a 1-inch circle punch? Use a quarter as a your guide: Trace around it on the wrong side of the paper, and cut it out.

PAPER-BEADED NECKLACE

Tiny rolls of scrap paper create delicate and colorful beads ready for stringing. For pennies, you can make millions. This project uses two paper beads for the necklace. But once you've rolled a few beads, you'll want to create an assortment of them for other jewelry ideas, too.

◢ **PROJECT SUMMARY** ◣

Paper beads are a great way to use bits of old scrapbook paper. Or, recycle junk mail and mags! Throw-away papers are loaded with colors and make the most unusual beads. Kids can easily make these paper beads too, just enlarge the pattern of the triangle for their tiny fingers

MAKING THE PAPER BEADS

You Will Need

Scraps of colorful paper	Toothpick
Scissors	Decoupage medium
White tacky glue	Paintbrush

1 Cut the paper into triangles that are about 1 inch or less across the bottom and about 2 inches high (photo A).

2 Place a dot of glue at the wide end of one triangle on the design side of the paper (photo B).

3 Lay a toothpick on the back side of the paper at the wide end of the triangle, and roll the triangle tightly around it, so that the glued side adheres to paper on the first turn (photo C).

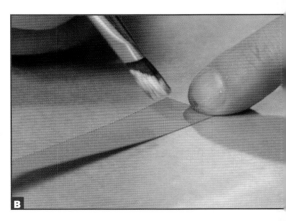

TIPS | DIY Network Crafts

RAINBOW OF CHOICES

Use matching colors on this necklace for an elegant look, or choose contrasting colors and different patterned beads for a bolder statement.

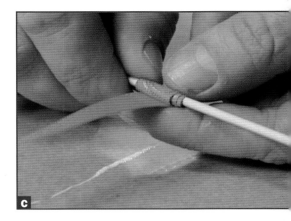

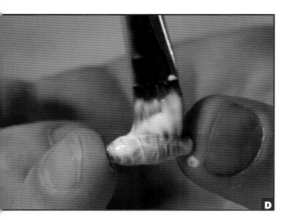

4 As you reach the last ½ inch of the paper (the pointed end), apply a drop of glue to hold the coil in place. Pull out the toothpick, and let the bead dry.

5 Repeat steps 2 through 4 to create the number of beads needed. (Two beads are used to make one necklace in the next project.)

6 Apply decoupage medium over each bead to create a glossy finish (photo D). Let dry before stringing.

TIPS | DIY Network Crafts

BEAD MANICURE

Don't have any decoupage medium on hand? Try using clear fingernail polish to gloss-up your beads. It doesn't give the same effect, but will coat your beads in a pinch!

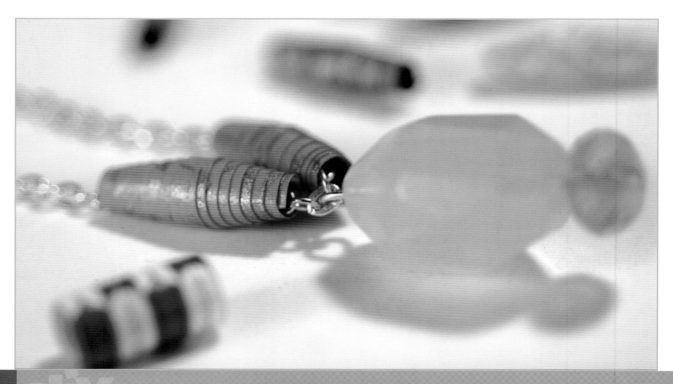

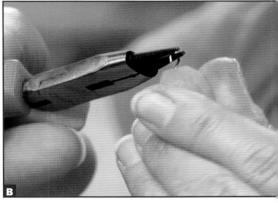

MAKING THE NECKLACE

You Will Need

Eye pin	18" chain
Small bead, cherry quartz	2 paper beads
Larger bead, pink quartz	Necklace clasp
Wire cutters	2 jump rings
Round-nosed pliers	

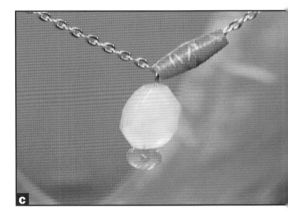

1 Make the drop for the necklace first: Thread the small and large bead onto the eye pin (photo A). Use wire cutters to trim the end of the eye pin to about ⅜ inch.

2 Use the round-nosed pliers to create a loop at the end of the eye pin (photo B).

3 Find the center of the chain. Open the loop on the eye pin with the pliers and attach it to the chain. Use the pliers to squeeze the pin loop closed again.

4 Thread one paper bead onto the chain on each side of the drop (photo C).

5 Attach the clasp with jump rings using round-nosed pliers (photo D).

CORDUROY PANTS PURSE

Back to school never looked so cool. Crop your old cords and fashion them into a carefree purse with tons of character to carry your essentials.

◢ **PROJECT SUMMARY** ◣

Make this purse by cropping your old cords, lining them with chic material, and adding pre-made purse handles. For extra fun and style, add patches to the bag, hippy style.

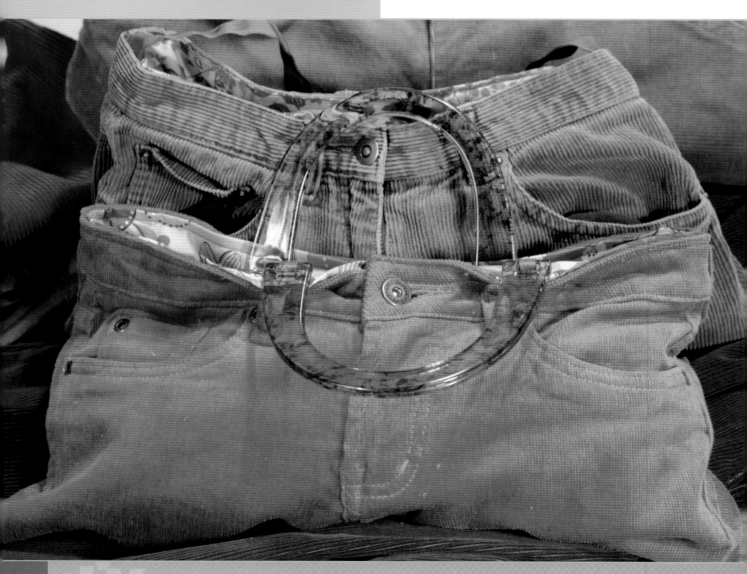

You Will Need

Old corduroy pants	Tape measure and chalk
Scissors	Iron
Straight pins	Purse handles
Sewing machine	Heavy-duty thread
Thread	Hand-sewing needle
½ yard lining fabric	

1 Cut off the legs of a pair of old corduroy pants at the hip line (photo A), just above the crotch seam, so that the bottom is open all the way across. Set the leg material aside for another project.

A

2 Turn the top of the pants inside out, and pin the cut-off edges together (photo B). Sew a seam along the edge with a ¾-inch seam allowance. Sew again over the first stitching for added strength Then, zigzag over the raw edge so that it won't ravel. (If your sewing machine has an overlock stitch, that's a great option for this edge.)

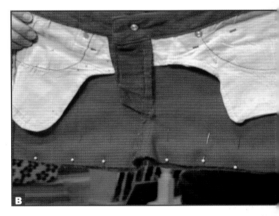

B

3 Measure the width (the inside of the waistband), and measure the height of the purse (photo C). Add 1 inch to the width measurement, and add 1½ inches to the height measurement. These new measurements are the dimensions of the lining.

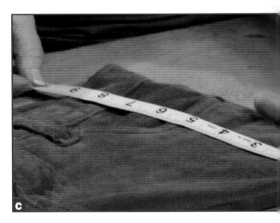

C

STAY COOL

Don't melt your lining fabric with a too-hot iron when you create the top fold! Care instructions for washing and ironing a fabric are usually on the bolt when you buy it. If you don't know the care instructions, be safe and set the iron to cool or warm for lining fabric. Natural fibers like cotton can tolerate a hotter temperature, but the synthetic content of most linings needs cooler temps.

4 Fold the lining fabric with right sides together. Using a tape measure and chalk, mark out the height and width dimensions figured in step 3 for the lining. Pin the thicknesses together inside the cutting line so the fabric won't shift as you cut, and then cut the lining to size.

5 Keeping right sides together, sew the sides of the lining first with a ½-inch seam allowance, and then sew the bottom.

6 For the top edge, fold the lining back ¾ inch and press it with an iron. Place the lining inside the purse without turning it—so the wrong side of the lining is against the wrong side of the purse. Pin the fold in place along the opening (photo D).

7 Adjust the length of stitch on your sewing machine according to the thickness of the corduroy—the thicker the fabric, the longer the stitch. Then, topstitch along the edge of the waistband on the outside of the purse (photo E) to secure the lining.

8 Center the handles on each side of the purse, and hand-stitch them into place using heavy-duty thread (photo F). For something different, try using recycled ribbon bits to create the handles.

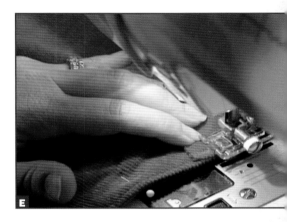

TIPS | DIY Network Crafts

ADDING A CLOSURE

To keep your valuables inside your bag, not tumbling out, add an easy closure by attaching a magnetic snap at the purse opening.

BOHEMIAN RINGS

Show your style with these handmade finger ornaments. Rummage through your old jewelry box or sewing basket and find treasures to recreate into jewels!

◤ **PROJECT SUMMARY** ◢

Use a round-nosed pliers and head pins to fashion dangles out of your old beads for this ring. You'll make at least one dangle for each loop on the ring blank. Find ring blanks—or ring bases—at a local bead shop or online.

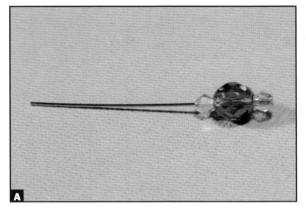

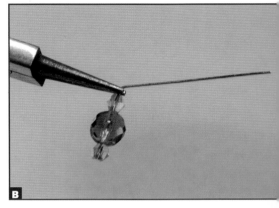

You Will Need

Beads from old necklaces or bracelets	Round-nosed pliers
Scissors	Wire cutters
Head pins	Looped ring blank

1 Cut apart old necklaces and bracelets, then sort the beads by shape and color. Choose the beads for your ring. Mixing and matching sizes, colors, and shapes will create an eclectic, bohemian-style ring. Or, use just one style of bead to create a modern chic ring.

2 To create the first dangle, thread the first beads onto a head pin. The size of the beads will determine how many you use (photo A).

3 Using the round-nosed pliers, bend the head pin to a 45-degree angle, just above the beads (photo B). Use the wire cutters to trim the pin to about ⅜ inch. With the round-nosed pliers, bend back the end of the pin to create a loop (photo C). This is the first dangle.

4 Open the loop on the dangle with the pliers to attach it to a loop on the ring blank (photo D). Create at least one dangle for each loop on the ring blank.

5 Repeat steps 2 through 4 to create more dangles until the ring blank is filled.

BUTTON RINGS

Show off your true crafty spirit with mismatched button rings. You will only need a few supplies to create these easy little gems.

◀ **PROJECT SUMMARY** ▶

To make this simple ring, you'll start with a ring blank and glue recycled buttons from old clothing onto it. That's all you need to make rings for every outfit!

You Will Need

Toothpick	Scrap of waxed paper
Heavy-duty glue	Adjustable ring blank (pad style)
2 fun buttons of different sizes	

1 Use a toothpick to apply glue to the back side of the smallest button (photo A). Set it in place on top of the larger button (photo B). Place the stack on a piece of waxed paper, and allow it to dry.

2 Place a drop of glue on the pad of the ring blank (photo C). Turn the button stack upside down and glue the ring base to the button stack (photo D). Allow to dry before wearing.

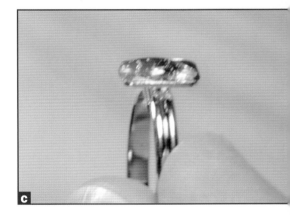

TIPS | DIY Network Crafts

FUNKY BUTTONS

Find great buttons on clothing at vintage stores and thrift shops. Some vintage stores have a button bin too, and sell unique buttons separately. Or, collect the "extra" buttons that come with your sweaters or your mom's suits and make rings with them.

BLEACHED ROCKER TEES

Transform an old T-shirt into a one-of-a-kind work of art. With a bleach pen and a little imagination you can create your own designer duds.

PROJECT SUMMARY

This project offers two options to create a design fora your T-shirt using self-adhesive vinyl: an outline template or a stencil template. You'll apply the design with a bleach pen by tracing whichever template you decide to make.

You Will Need

100% cotton T-shirt (medium to dark color), prewashed
Folded newspaper, several inches thick
T-shirt design
Clear self-adhesive vinyl (such as shelf paper)
Permanent marker
Craft knife or scissors
Bleach pen
Masking tape

1 Insert the stack of newspaper into the T-shirt, separating the front of the shirt from the back. This will keep the bleach applied to the design from bleeding onto the back of the shirt.

2 Use an outlining template, as in the next step, to apply the design to the shirt, or skip to step 6 to make a stencil template. The T-shirt shown uses an outlining template for the guitar and a stencil template for the letter "g."

3 To create an outlining template: Use a printed image, or a design of your own (such as the guitar shape here). Place the image on top of a piece of self-adhesive vinyl, and trace the outline onto the vinyl with a permanent marker (photo A).

4 Cut out the template and remove the paper backing from the vinyl. Lay the vinyl, adhesive side down, into position on the T-shirt. Press the template carefully to the fabric, making sure that there are no air bubbles or loose areas.

5 Using the bleach pen, trace around the edges of the template onto the T-shirt (photo B). Use a continuous line, polka dots, or whatever style you prefer, to mark the outline.

6 To create a stencil template: For a stencil image, be sure to choose a high-contrast, black-and-white design. (You need to be able to see the design through the vinyl in order to make the stencil.) Cut a rectangle of self-adhesive vinyl a few inches bigger in each direction than your design. Using masking tape, tape the image to the paper backing of the vinyl. With the vinyl side up, use a permanent marker to trace the image onto the vinyl, drawing the outline as well as the inside areas of the design. Cut along the lines using a craft knife, saving the inside areas of the design to apply to the shirt as well.

7 Carefully peel the protective backing off of the vinyl. Place it into position on the T-shirt. Peel and apply the inside areas of the design to the T-shirt as well. Press the vinyl carefully to the fabric, pressing out any air bubbles or loose areas.

8 Using the bleach pen, liberally apply bleach to the cut-away portions of the stencil (photo C). Allow the bleach to sit and soak into the fabric. This happens quickly—you will see it bleaching.

9 When the bleach has the desired effect, remove the newspaper and rinse the shirt in cold water to stop the bleaching. Then, pull the vinyl stencils off and wash the T-shirt in a washing machine with mild detergent to remove any residual bleach. Line or tumble dry, and wear it in style!

TIPS | DIY Network Crafts

PROTECT YOUR HANDS
Bleach can be hard on your skin and dry it out—read the precautions on your bleach pen and wash your hands after any direct contact with bleach.

VELVET & LEATHER BELTS & BRACELETS

Throw back to the era of '70s rock with easy vintage-style accessories by revamping an old belt and bangle bracelet with a little velvet ribbon. This duo will give you style!

◢ PROJECT SUMMARY ◢

Give a hip retro look to a plain old belt in this project by punching holes in the leather and weaving velvet ribbon through them. Then, create a cool matching accessory by wrapping an old bracelet in the same velvet ribbon.

MAKING THE BELT

You Will Need

Old leather belt	Scissors
Leather hole punch	Heavy-duty glue
Velvet ribbon, 2" longer than the belt	

1 Use a leather punch to create holes down the center or along both edges of the belt (photo A). Space the holes about 1 inch apart, or adjust to your taste.

2 Weave the ribbon, velvet side up, through the punched holes from one end to the other of the belt (photo B).

3 Trim the ribbon, leaving a 1-inch tail on the back side at both ends (photo C).

4 Working on the back side of the belt and using a heavy-duty glue, glue back the ends of the ribbon to the leather. Press the ribbon firmly to the belt, and allow the glue to dry.

MAKING THE BRACELET

You Will Need

Thick plastic dangle bracelet

Velvet ribbon in matching color

Glue

Scissors

1 Glue one end of the ribbon to the bracelet. Press it firmly, and allow it to dry (photo A).

2 Wrap the ribbon in and out, around the bracelet, crossing the width of the band at an angle. Glue the edge of the ribbon to the bracelet as you wrap (photo B).

3 When you have completed the circle, trim the end of the ribbon, and secure it with a drop of glue (photo C). Press the ribbon end to the bracelet firmly, and allow the glue to dry completely before wearing.

A

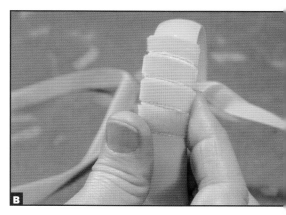

B

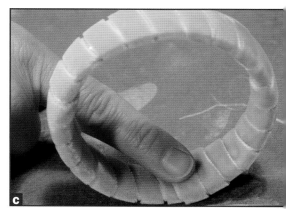

C

TIE-DYED SLIP

Go knotty and slip into some dye to create this flirty, sparkly, dainty slip. Re-styled vintage never looked so hip. Use an old slip of your own or find one at a secondhand store. Then, choose a color of dye that becomes you, or create your own color by mixing it up!

◢◤ PROJECT SUMMARY ◢◤

See how easy tie-dyeing can be with this project! Use rubber bands to bind an old slip into sections and immerse in a dye bath. Rinse, cut off the rubber bands, and you have a great retro striped look--up and down or side to side. Be sure to wear rubber gloves and old clothes for this project!

You Will Need

Pale-colored nylon or silk slip

Water

Rubber bands

Fabric dye

Old dishpan or bucket for dye bath

Rubber gloves

Washing machine

Mild detergent

Sequins or rhinestones

Jewel glue

1 If this is a new slip, wash it according to the label to remove any sizing.

2 To prepare the slip for dye, saturate it with water and wring out any excess. This will allow the dye to distribute evenly.

3 Lay the slip out and fold it up, accordion fashion (photo A). In the example, the slip was folded top to bottom to result in vertical stripes. If you fold your slip side-to-side accordion style, you'll create horizontal stripes.

4 Bind off the slip into 6 sections using rubber bands (photo B). Loop the rubber bands tightly. The dye will not go into the area binded with the rubber bands—which creates the tie-dye effect.

A

B

5 Mix the dye in the dishpan or bucket according to the manufacturer's instructions. Wearing rubber gloves, submerge the slip into the dye bath (photo C). Allow the slip to remain in the dye for the time recommended by the manufacturer's instructions.

6 Remove the slip from the dye and rinse it until the water runs clear. Cut or remove the rubber bands (photo D) and check out the design you created!

7 Wash the slip in the washing machine with a mild detergent to remove residual dye (photo E). Allow the slip to dry. Add sequins, rhinestones, or other trims and embellishments with jewel glue.

8 After washing the slip in the washing machine, run the empty washer through a cycle with bleach to remove any residual dye that could stain lighter clothes in the next load.

CUSTOM COLORING

Want a color all your own? Make any color in the spectrum by experimenting with mixing dyes. Some dyes come with recipes for mixing custom colors, or check the manufacturer's website for ideas.

Here are some mixing basics. Just about any color can be created by mixing three basic colors: cyan, magenta, and yellow. Equal parts of magenta and yellow make red; yellow and cyan make green; and cyan and magenta make purple. Less of magenta and more of yellow make orange; some magenta, some cyan, and more yellow make brown. A bit of black added to any mixture makes the same color darker.

Too many colors in the mix may end up looking like mud. It's a good idea to check your custom color on a scrap of similar fabric before dyeing your slip.

ROCKABILLY WRIST CUFF

Get ready to slice, dice, and stitch old jeans into cool custom wrist cuffs. One pair of jeans can yield a few cuffs so grab some fun patches and get creative. Add your own attitude to this cuff with a patch that makes a statement or a whimsical one that just says fun!

◢ PROJECT SUMMARY ◢

You'll need a snap setter for this project—an inexpensive tool that will make installing snaps a snap! This wrist cuff is made of a strip of denim from old jeans. You'll fray the edges with a pin, apply a decorative patch, and use your snap setter and a hammer to install three snazzy snaps to keep it in place.

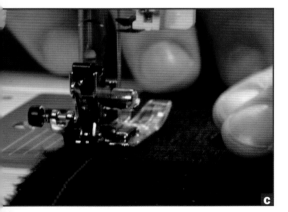

You Will Need

Tape measure	Straight pins
Old jeans	Patch or scrap of fabric
Scissors	Chalk
Sewing machine	Three heavy-duty snaps
Topstitching thread	Snap setter and hammer

1 Measure around your wrist and add 1 inch (photo A) for the length of the wrist cuff. This will allow space for snaps.

2 Cut two strips from the width of the leg of an old pair of jeans. Make the strips 3-inches wide and as long as the measurement determined in step 1 (photo B).

3 With wrong sides together and right sides facing out, topstitch around the outer edge of the strips with a $\frac{1}{4}$-inch seam allowance (photo C)

4 Fray the edges of the denim using a pin, pulling threads out along the edges to give it a short fringe.

5 Center a patch or decorative scrap of fabric onto the cuff. Pin it in place (Photo D). Using a contrasting color of thread, topstitch the patch to the cuff (photo E).

6 Mark the placement for 3 snaps on the edge of the cuff: Fold the two ends back over themselves and mark the locations with a piece of chalk (photo F).

7 Lay the cuff across your wrist in the way you will wear it. The edge of the cuff at the outside of your wrist is the edge for the top portion, or cover, of the snaps. (This is the right edge on the right wrist, left edge on the left wrist.) The other end will wrap underneath it with the bottom portion of the snaps.

8 Use the snap setter to attach the snaps (photo G), following the instructions on the package.

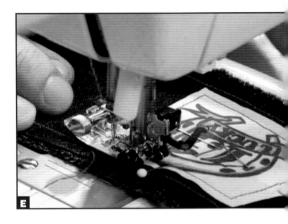

TIPS | DIY Network Crafts

SUPER FRAY

After making the cuff, run it through the washer and dryer to create a super-frayed look.

SEAM ALLOWANCE

A "seam allowance" is the distance from the edge of the material to the stitch of the seam. A standard seam allowance for sewing clothing is ⅝ inch. When topstitching or sewing crafts, seam allowances vary according to the need. This wrist cuff calls for a ¼-inch seam allowance to keep the stitching close to the edge of the cuff for visual appeal and wearability. Your sewing machine plate may have markings to denote ⅛-inch increments for seam allowances to help you feed your fabric through evenly. Use the seam allowance specified in the sewing instructions, or if no width is given, sew with a ⅝-inch seam.

2

Decorate

If pictures say a thousand words, think of what your friends and family will say when they see the creative ways you've displayed your photos. If you're like most people, you have boxes and boxes of family photos. Well, we've thought up some funky fresh ways to frame them, showcase them, even wear them. Turn the pages in this chapter to see our take on scrapbooking.

Cathie   Steve

FOLK ART HUBCAP CANDELABRA

Folk art and fancy free—your front room or backyard will bloom with character and funky style with this candelabra.

▰ PROJECT SUMMARY ▰

Paint a simple hubcap and adorn it with bits and baubles to create a hanging candelabra. Use recycled beads and baubles from old jewelry to create the beaded drops. Don't worry if they don't match…that adds character! Find the chain for hanging at a hardware store—the same kind used for hanging lamps or plants.

You Will Need

Heavy-duty cleaner or degreaser	Polyurethane spray gloss
Water	Fishing line
Old metal hubcap	Scissors
Painter's tape or masking tape	Beads, charms, crystals, shells, or baubles
Metal primer spray paint	Glass candle plate
Acrylic paints, various colors	Epoxy for glass
Paintbrushes, various sizes	Pliers
Pencil	Heavy-duty chain (as for lamps)
Lightweight sandpaper	Pillar candle
Acrylic paint, cream colored	

1 Use heavy-duty cleaner or a degreasing agent to clean the hubcap thoroughly. Allow to dry completely.

2 Use painter's tape or masking tape to cover any areas of the hubcap that will not be painted (photo A). Then, spraypaint the hubcap with the metal primer, and allow it to dry.

3 Paint a base coat onto the hubcap using a medium-sized paintbrush and various paint colors. Allow the hubcap to dry.

4 Paint additional details like stripes and blocks of color over the base coat, using various colors again (photo B). Layer the colors for added dimension. Allow the paint to dry between each layer.

TIPS | DIY Network Crafts

PERFECT POLKA DOTS
Try using the eraser end of a pencil dipped in paint to apply easy polka dots to your folk art design.

5 Let the design dry completely. Then, lightly sand the surface of the paint to add texture to the design.

6 Mix a small amount of water with cream-colored paint to create a milk wash. Using quick strokes, paint the wash over the design areas on the hubcap (photo C). Let dry.

7 Spray clear gloss polyurethane over the entire hubcap to seal the design and add sheen.

8 Decorate the hubcap with beaded drops. To make the drops, cut a 24-inch piece of fishing line. Tie a small bead in the center of the line and bring the loose ends back together. Thread the beads and baubles onto the double thickness of fishing line to make about 6 inches of strung beads. Tie a knot above the beads on the line and leave the extra length for tying the drop to the hubcap.

9 Repeat step 8 for as many drops as desired. Add charms, crystals, shells, or other baubles as well. Tie the strands to the underside of the hubcap, and clip off any extra fishing line (photo C).

10 Using epoxy, secure the glass candle plate to the center of the hubcap, and allow it to dry.

11 Measure the circumference of the hubcap, and mark the edge of the cap into thirds. Cut three sections of heavy-duty chain to length for hanging. Using pliers, open a link of the chain and attach the chain to the hubcap at each mark so that the hubcap is balanced. Hang the candelabra, place a candle in the center, and light (photo D).

LIGHT READING CENTERPIECE

Transform old books into a centerpiece perfect for a book club or the avid readers in your life. Simple and whimsical, this centerpiece will be the star of the table.

PROJECT SUMMARY

Build this centerpiece with old books and hot glue. You will need a drill and hole saw bit to make cuts to hold candles. Make sure the bit you use is slightly larger than the diameter of the votive candleholders.

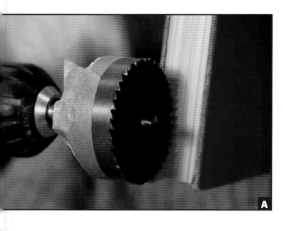

You Will Need

3 old books (1½" to 2" thick)	Binder clips
Masking tape	Decorative ribbon
Hole saw carbon drill bit	Hot glue gun
Drill	Hot glue
Gel medium	Paint
Paintbrush	3 glass votive holders
Waxed paper	3 votive candles

1 Choose 3 thick books for the centerpiece and stack them in the order desired. Working with the top book, measure its thickness and divide that in half.

2 Mark the measurement from step 1 onto the hole saw bit with masking tape (photo A) to provide a gauge for drilling the proper depth into the book.

3 Drill 3 holes into the top book, through the cover and into the pages, using the hole saw bit with the masking tape gauge (photo B). Space the holes evenly or randomly, whichever you prefer. Remove any loose pieces with your fingers.

4 Paint the inside of the drilled holes with the gel medium, including the sides and bottom of the holes (photo C). Allow to dry. This will hold the drilled book together and create a finished look.

TIPS | DIY Network Crafts

CHOOSING CENTERPIECE BOOKS

Here's an instance in which you may want to choose a book by its cover! Look for books with color and flair—those that have great covers or interesting edges on the pages. Books with gold edges make beautiful centerpieces!

5 Working with all 3 books, apply the gel medium inside the front cover, back cover and around all side edges of the book. This will seal all the pages together. Wrap the books with waxed paper to prevent sticking and clamp them with large binder clips (photo D). Allow to dry.

6 Decorate the books with ribbon, using hot glue to secure it. Or paint over the dried gel medium to add color (photo E).

7 Glue the books into a stack using hot glue (photo F). (Make sure the drilled book is on top!) Angle the books in different directions to add interest to the piece.

8 Fit the candleholders into the holes and add candles. Use additional ribbon, bows, or charms around the base of the candleholders or added to the edges of the books.

D

E

F

FIRE & ICE SCULPTURE

Combine fire and ice to create one-of-a-kind organic centerpieces that are sure to create a mood, be it for large gatherings or a more intimate occasion.

▰ **PROJECT SUMMARY** ▰

The mold for this project is simply a recycled juice carton that's peeled away and discarded when its job is done! Create a centerpiece to fit a theme or just to express yourself.

You Will Need

Half-gallon cardboard milk/juice container	Water
Scissors	Dried flowers, fruits, small flowers
Tall candle	Freezer
Masking tape	Shallow bowl

1 Thoroughly clean the carton with soap and water. Use scissors to remove the top (photo A), cutting the carton to about the height of the candle, or less, so it's easier to work with.

2 Center the candle in the empty container—either a pillar candle or a taper candle will work. Just use masking tape to secure the candle to the edge of the carton to keep it centered and upright, if needed.

3 Add water to the carton to the desired height of the ice. A good height is ½ to ¾ of the way up the candle (photo B).

4 Add decorative objects around the candle within the carton, such as dried flowers, fruits, or small fresh flowers (photo C).

5 Freeze the carton overnight, or until the ice is a solid block. Remove the centerpiece from the carton by dipping it quickly in warm water and then peeling away the paper carton (photo D).

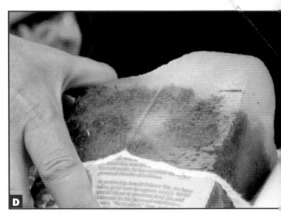

6 Display the centerpiece in a shallow bowl with additional greenery or flowers around the edge. Check the bowl periodically while your candle is on display to make sure it doesn't overflow as the ice melts. Depending on room temperature the centerpiece may last 4 to 8 hours.

TIPS | DIY Network Crafts

A PLAYFUL TWIST

If wall fruits and flowers are not your style, try the same technique using small plastic toys or other figures. Stack them in the water or suspend them with fishing line tied to masking tape across the top of the container.

METAL PIPE CANDLEHOLDERS

New meets old when you combine metal pipe and patina to create this unusual candleholder and light up your table with tons of character.

◢ PROJECT SUMMARY ◣

Use metal pipe and fittings to build this candleholder, and then paint on patina kit solutions to create an age-old look. Use different patina finishes to make several to display together.

You Will Need

¾" metal pipe, threaded on each end	Patina kit
¾" metal flange	Paintbrushes
1" metal coupling	Tin foil scrap

1 Thread the flange onto the pipe for a base. Attach the coupling onto the top of the pipe for the candle.

2 Use a paintbrush to apply the copper portion of the faux patina kit to the entire surface of the candleholder (photo A). Allow it to dry.

3 Apply the patina green antiquing solution to the entire candleholder (photo B). The patina will begin to take effect in just a few minutes (photo C). To add more patina, just add more antiquing solution.

4 Form a piece of tin foil around the candle's base for fit, and insert a candle into the coupling.

TIPS | DIY Network Crafts

NATURAL CHARACTER

For added character, use old pipe pieces rather than new. Patina or spraypaint right over any existing corrosion or wear.

WHAT IS PATINA?

By definition, "patina" is a thin, colored layer on the surface of some metals and minerals caused by corrosion. The most common example is the green layer that covers copper and bronze as it ages. This effect can be recreated on just about any surface—metal or non-metal—with patina kits sold in craft stores. The kits include a metal surfacer (fine metal particles suspended in a sealing compound) used to coat the object, and a patina solution to oxidize the reactive metal surfacer. The oxidation creates the visual effect of patina. Some kits also come with tinting solutions—a dye-based finish to add color and contrast to the patina finish.

HAWAIIAN LUMINARY

Dress up plain cylindrical vases into vibrant candleholders to light up your evening. Decorate like the Aloha state, or cut out pictures and drawings from old magazines and books for retro appeal.

PROJECT SUMMARY

Use your own color laser printer to create a print of a fun Hawaiian fabric or other material for this luminary, or make color prints at a local copy shop.

You Will Need

Clear cylindrical vase	White primer paint
Tape measure	Glossy decoupage medium
Hawaiian fabric	Waxed paper
Color laser copier	Gold acrylic paint
Scissors or paper cutter	Clear varnish (optional)
Ruler	Votive candle with holder
Sponge paintbrush	

1 Measure the cylindrical vase from top to bottom and subtract ½ inch. Then, measure around the cylinder, subtract ½ inch, and divide by 2. These are the height and width measurements, respectively, for the color copies.

2 Make two color laser copies of Hawaiian fabrics. Size the copies to the dimensions determined in step 1. Use scissors or a paper cutter to trim both copies as needed (photo A).

3 Using a sponge brush, paint the sides and bottom of the vase with a coat of primer, and allow it to dry (photo B).

4 Using a sponge brush, apply a liberal amount of decoupage medium to the vase.

5 Place one copied image, printed side down, onto a sheet of waxed paper and apply a liberal amount of decoupage medium to the back of the image. Turn the image over and apply a liberal amount of decoupage medium to the printed side of the image as well.

6 Position the image on the vase about ¼ inch from the top edge. Use your fingers to smooth out any air bubbles. Follow with the sponge brush to smooth out any finger marks in the decoupage (photo C).

7 Repeat steps four and five with the other color copy, positioning the image ¼ inch from the top edge and centering it on the backside of the vase. Allow the decoupage to dry overnight.

8 Using gold acrylic paint, paint the top and bottom edges of the cylinder. Allow to dry. Then, invert the cylinder and paint the bottom primed area as well. Allow the base to dry before continuing.

9 If desired, coat the entire vase with clear varnish as well. Allow to dry.

10 Insert a tea light candle into the luminary. Use a candle with a metal band or glass holder to keep the hot wax contained. Then, clean up is a snap, and you can use the colorful piece as a vase as well as a luminary.

A

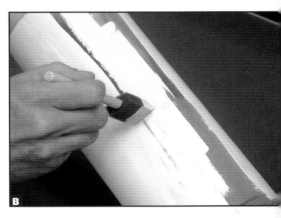

B

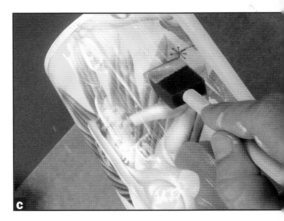

C

TIPS | DIY Network Crafts

WHY NOT INK JET?

The finish on a laser copy will withstand the moisture and materials used to make the luminaries, while the image on an ink jet copy may run. If needed, take your fabric to an office supply store or copy center to make color laser copies.

3

Give

Creating homemade gifts that your friends and family are sure to love is as easy as a few snips and stitches. The best part about giving is the smile on someone's face as he or she opens your gift, and knowing that you made the gift yourself makes even more special. In this chapter, we give some crafty ideas for making your gifts even more memorable.

Cathie   *Steve*

FLORAL BUTTON CARDS

Next time you want to send a special note, create your own handmade fanciful greeting with just a few stitches and a couple of old buttons.

◀ PROJECT SUMMARY ▶

Stitch flowers onto a greeting card using embroidery thread and buttons in this project, finishing it off with ribbon. Be sure to use flat buttons so the card can fit into its envelope for mailing or hand delivery.

You Will Need

5 x 7 card, blank	Embroidery floss
Cardstock scrap	Fun flat buttons
Scissors	Ribbon scrap
Pencil	Paper glue or tacky glue
Small needle	

1 Trim the cardstock scrap to be slightly smaller than the blank card (photo A). The design will be embroidered onto the card stock, then glued to the blank card.

2 Use a pencil to sketch out the stems of the flowers on the card, if desired, or just sew them freehand in the next step.

3 To stitch the stems and leaves, separate the embroidery floss and thread two strands of the floss onto the needle. Make a knot on the end of the thread. Insert the needle from the backside of the cardstock through to the front. Use a split stitch to create the stems (photo B). Add leaves, if desired, with a satin stitch (photo C, next page). Glue the buttons onto the tops of the stems (photo D, next page).

A

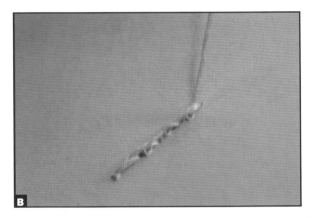

B

4 Measure across the top of the card and add ½ inch. Cut 2 pieces of ribbon to that measurement. Place a bead of glue across the back of the ribbons, and attach them across the top and bottom of the card stock (photo E), wrapping ¼ inch around the edge of the card on both sides.

5 Center the stitched paper over the blank card and glue it into place (photo F).

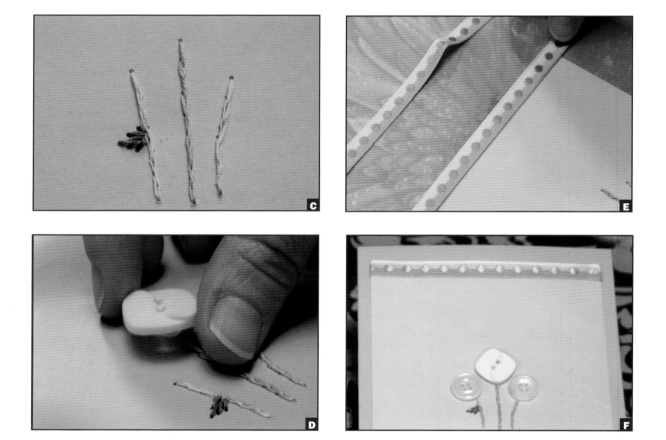

IT'S A STITCH

Split Stitch: To create a split stitch, make your first stitch on the card, following the sketched line. Then, make a small backstitch, bringing the needle up through the sewn thread.

Satin Stitch: Work straight stitches closely together across the shape you want to fill. Take care to keep the edge even. If you are following an outline marked on the paper, take your stitches to the outside of the line so that the mark does not show on the finished design.

RECYCLED GIFT BAG & FANCY WRAPPED GIFT

Need a fanciful wrap for a great gift? With a few punches of scrap paper, recycle an old shopping bag and create a designer-wrapped look in no time.

◢ **PROJECT SUMMARY** ◣

Use a flower paper punch to design your own rhinestone-studded wrapping paper. Be sure to buy rhinestones that are small enough for the center of your punched flowers. Then, remake an old shopping bag with decorative paper and clip art or greeting card cutouts.

WRAPPED GIFT

You Will Need

Gift and wrapping paper	Gem glue
Decorative floral paper punches	Rhinestones
	Glue stick
Decorative paper scraps	Ribbon

1 Wrap the gift in the wrapping paper. Plain paper works best to set off the creative, fun embellishments you'll add in the next steps.

2 Use decorative punches to create floral shapes from the decorative scrap paper (photo A). Apply gem glue to the small rhinestones, and press them to the centers of the punched flower shapes (photo B). Allow to dry.

3 Secure the floral shapes to the wrapped gift using a glue stick. Place the shapes in a random pattern all over the box (photo C). Finally, add a decorative bow (photo D).

GIFT BAG

You Will Need

Paper shopping bag with handles	Glue stick
Decorative paper scraps	Clip art or old greeting cards
Scissors	

1 Measure the printed logo, if any, on the shopping bag. Cut decorative paper into an oval or circle large enough to cover the print on the bag.

2 Use a glue stick to coat the back of the cutout, and press it into place on the bag. This will be the backdrop for decorative images in the next step.

3 Cut out clip art or images from old greeting cards. Use a glue stick to adhere the cutouts to the decorative paper on the bag (photo A).

TIPS | DIY Network Crafts

ELEGANT BAG HANDLES

If the handles on the bag are not so cute, just snip them off and thread decorative ribbon through the sides for handles.

PERFECT CIRCLE

Need a perfect circle? Just place a bowl of the appropriate size onto the paper and trace around it.

VEGAS DICE BRACELET

You won't have to gamble on your friends liking this gift—it's a sure thing. And, for a matching necklace, just repeat the pattern until you reach the desired length.

Thread dice and beads onto wire for this hip bracelet. Instructions on how to drill the dice are included here, or simply buy pre-drilled dice.

You Will Need

Vise	2 crimp beads
6 to 9 dice	Flat-nosed pliers
Drill and ⅛" bit	Seed beads, medium size, silver
Jewelry beading wire	Seed beads, small, black
Wire cutters	Decorative beads, medium size
Bracelet clasp	

1 Attach the vise to your work surface and secure the jaws of the vise onto one die. Drill a hole in the center point of the die, going halfway through (photo A). Flip the die over and drill at the center point from the other side as well, drilling through to the first hole. Repeat for all of the dice (photo B)—use six to nine dice, depending on their size.

2 Cut a piece of beading wire the length for the bracelet, adding enough wire to attach the clasp. Thread a crimp bead onto one end of the wire. Add the clasp, then fold the wire back and through the crimp bead. Crimp the bead closed with flat-nosed pliers (photo C).

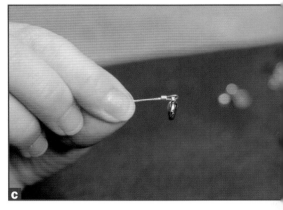

3 To add the beads and dice, begin by threading a silver seed bead, then add a die (photo D). Tuck the tail end of the wire through the beads as you go. Add beads and dice alternately until the wire is full.

4 When you reach the desired length, attach the ring portion of the clasp as described in step 2 (photo E). Tuck the tail end of the wire back through the beads to finish the bracelet.

PERSONALIZED COAT HANGERS

Giving a robe or special dress as a gift?
Transform an old wooden hanger into a
designer showstopper to go with it!

▷ **PROJECT SUMMARY** ◁

Give an old hanger a coat of paint and spruce it up
with designs cut from old gift wrap. Then, cover it
with decoupage and varnish for a nice sheen.

You Will Need

Wooden clothes hanger	Detail scissors
Fine grit sandpaper	Decoupage medium
Damp cloth	Spray varnish
Masking tape	Ribbon scrap
Craft paints and brushes	Small rhinestones (optional)
Stickers	Gem glue (optional)
Recycled gift wrap	

1 Lightly sand the clothes hanger, and wipe away the dust with a damp cloth.

2 Cover the metal hook completely with tape. Choose the base color for the hanger, and coat the hanger on both sides with craft paint. Allow to dry.

3 On one side of the hanger, spell out a name in stickers or paint the letters by hand, if desired. Add other designs by painting stripes, polka dots, or squiggles in other colors (photo A). Use various sizes of paintbrushes for effect. For perfect polka dots, try dipping the eraser end of a pencil in craft paint and dot onto the hanger. Allow to dry.

4 Cut images or designs from a piece of old gift wrap, making them small enough to fit on the face of the hanger. Use a detail scissors to cut around the images if needed.

5 On the other side of the hanger, apply decoupage medium. Place the paper cutouts onto the decoupage medium on the hanger (photo B). Add cutouts until the surface is filled to your liking. Use your fingers to press out any air bubbles.

6 Apply a top coat of decoupage medium over the cutouts (photo C). Allow to dry.

7 Coat all sides of the hanger with spray varnish. Allow to dry, and remove the tape from the hook. Tie a bow around the metal hook, and use gem glue to attach small rhinestones to the hanger, if desired.

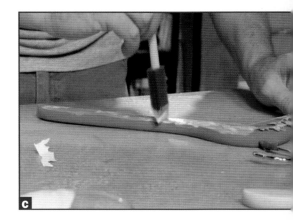

TIPS | DIY Network Crafts

HAPPY HANGERS

For kids, make a few different hangers—one for each coat. A fun hanger takes the chore out of hanging up coats!

SHEER LIP GLOSS & FUNKY CASES

Rummage through old makeup drawers and have fun creating new sheer lip colors and personalized cases—from leopard print and pin-up girls to polka-dot fun.

◣ **PROJECT SUMMARY** ◢

Use lipstick and lip balm to mix up tons of different shades of lip gloss, and then remake a makeup compact to hold the gloss. Use the squeeze-tube style of lip balm for ease in this project.

You Will Need

Old makeup (eye shadow) compact with a mirror	Paper glue
⅛ stick colored lipstick	Decorative paper punches
Lip balm	Rhinestones
Sandwich bag	Gem glue
Decorative paper	

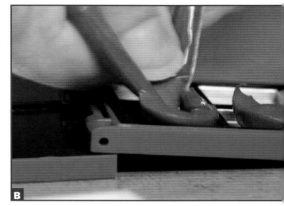

1 Remove any residual eye shadow or makeup from the compact and clean it out well, washing with soap and water. (Use a toothpick for corners and edges, if needed.) Allow to dry thoroughly.

2 Cut off the used end of the lipstick and discard. Then, place a small portion of the unused lipstick and a small portion of the lip balm into a sandwich bag. For super-sheer lip gloss, use just a dab of lipstick. Seal the bag and work it with your fingers to blend the contents (photo A). Blend in additional gloss or lipstick as needed for the desired color

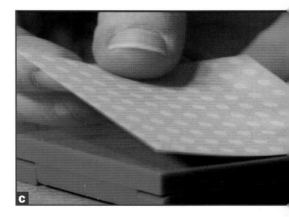

3 Snip a corner of the bag and pipe (like frosting) the lip gloss into the makeup section of the compact (photo B).

4 To personalize the case, apply decorative paper to the top of the compact with paper glue (photo C). Then, glue on punched paper designs. Accent them with paper and rhinestones applied with gem glue, if desired (photo D). Or, you can customize your compact with a monogram or a fun photo instead.

TIPS | DIY Network Crafts

MINI CASES

Small pillboxes are great for lip gloss too!
Find them at a dollar store or container store.

INDIAN POTPOURRI POMANDERS

Create scented pomanders that fill a room with bright cheery color and rich exotic scents.

◣ **PROJECT SUMMARY** ◢

Use a simple papier-mâché technique to make these potpourri-scented pomanders, using raquet-balls as a base. Experiment with different colors and textures to personalize the surface of these fun little gifts.

You Will Need

Small rubber ball (such as a racquetball)	Craft knife
Petroleum Jelly	Awl
Newspaper	Small cork
White glue	Primer
Disposable drinking cups	Craft paint
Rubber bands	Potpourri and spices
Permanent marker	Ribbon
Pencil	Small crystal rhinestones

A

1 Coat each rubber ball with a thin layer of petroleum jelly to allow the papier-mâché to slide nicely off the mold later (photo A).

2 Make a glue solution of one part white glue and one part water. Tear newspaper into small strips, coat with the glue solution, and wrap around the ball (photo B). Coat each ball with six layers of the papier-mâché. Set each ball in a disposable cup and allow to dry.

3 Stretch a rubber band around the center of each ball, and use a permanent marker to draw a dashed line along the rubber band as a cutting guide for the center line (photo C).

B

TIPS | DIY Network Crafts

C

SPICE IT UP

Use traditional Indian spices such as fennel (sweet licorice scent), star anise (black licorice scent), and cloves (rich and aromatic). Or, use lavender and chamomile for a relaxing mixture.

4 Using a craft knife, carefully cut through the paper along the dotted line (photo D). Peel each paper shell from the rubber ball. Set the shells aside and allow the interiors to dry completely (photo E).

5 Align the edges of the dry halves together, and re-join them with glue. Cover the joints with thin layers of papier-mâché, and allow them to dry again.

6 Use two rubber bands to quarter off the ball. Use the awl to carefully pierce multiple holes in each partition of the paper ball (photo F). Make a larger hole at the bottom of each ball to fit the cork that will plug it (photo G).

7 Apply a coat of primer to the paper balls, and allow to dry. Then paint with craft paint, being careful that the paint does not fill the awled holes. Allow time between each coat for the paint to dry completely (photo H).

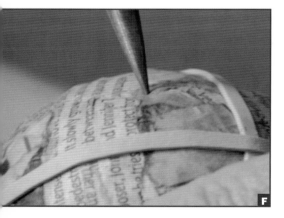

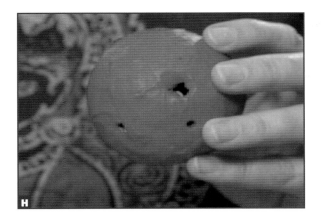

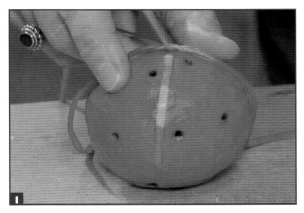

8 Fill each ball with a mixture of potpourri and spices through the larger hole. Plug the hole with the cork.

9 Secure a decorative ribbon to each ball with dots of white glue (photo I). Add a few rhinestones for added sparkle, and hang (photo J).

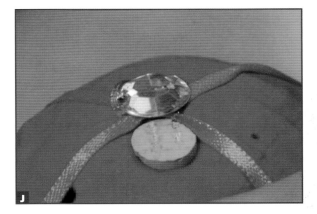

WINE BOTTLE SOAP DISPENSER

Recycle a wine bottle for the cutest housewarming gift—with a little clay and a lot of soap, your friends can have the coolest kitchen.

▨ **PROJECT SUMMARY** ▧

Decorate an old wine bottle with polymer clay, top the bottle with a spout, and fill with your favorite kitchen soap. You'll need to use an oven to bake the clay for this gift.

You Will Need

Wine bottle	Alphabet stamps
Rubbing alcohol	Oven
Paper towel	Quick-hold craft glue
Pearl polymer clay	Fine-tipped permanent marker
Blue polymer clay	
Clay roller (or pasta machine)	Dish soap
Drinking glass	Liquor pour spout

1 Thoroughly wash the wine bottle, soaking it in water to remove the label. Use rubbing alcohol and a paper towel to remove any excess glue or gum left by the label.

2 Knead both polymer clays, following the manufacturer's instructions for your brand.

3 Roll a thin layer of pearl polymer clay about ⅛- to ¼-inch thick using either a clay rolling pin or a pasta machine (photo A). This is the base of the "soap label."

4 Cut out a circle of clay with the drinking glass (photo B). Give it a bit of a twist to press it through the clay. Remove the glass, and clean up the edges of the clay, if desired.

5 Use rubber stamps to press the word "s-o-a-p" across the clay circle. Clean the stamps right away to remove any clay residue.

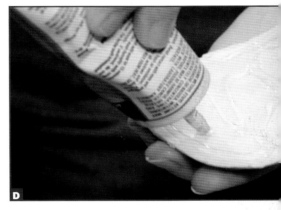

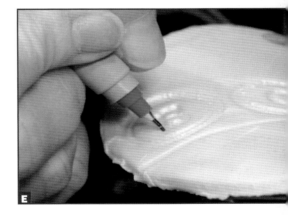

6 Create small "soap bubbles" with the blue polymer clay by rolling small pieces of clay in your hands and flattening them with your fingers. Apply them onto the clay soap label (photo C).

7 Press the clay label onto the wine bottle, fitting it to the curve of the bottle. Place in the oven, and bake according to the clay manufacturer's instructions—usually about 15 to 20 minutes. Turn off the oven, and use oven mitts to remove the bottle from the oven. Let cool.

8 Remove the baked clay from the bottle and apply quick-hold glue to the back of the clay (photo D). Glue to the bottle in the desired position.

9 Use a thin permanent marker to add additional detail by tracing over the letters on the clay (photo E). Fill the bottle with soap, and cap it off with a pour spout.

VINTAGE MOROCCAN SOY CANDLES

Add a glow to any room or any friend's heart when you give this candle as a gift.

▤ PROJECT SUMMARY ▥

Recycle Moroccan tea glasses in this project by filling them with clean-burning soy wax and a favorite fragrance. Compared to traditional soap making techniques, glycerin soap is quick and simple to do—just melt the blocks, stir in your favorite fragrance and pour into molds.

You Will Need

Moroccan tea glasses	Large pan and water
Large glass measuring cup	Stovetop
Soy container wax	Candle thermometer
Cotton-cored wick	Oven mitts
Metal wick base	Stirring spoon
Pencil	Essential oil or fragrance oil

1 To determine the amount of wax needed, fill the tea glass with water. Pour the water into a measuring cup and note the amount. Dry the glass thoroughly. Calculate the wax needed for each candle—16 ounces of soy wax will make 2¼ cups of melted wax.

2 Attach the metal wick base to one end of the wick, following the instructions on the package (photo A). Tie the other end of the wick to the middle of a pencil, and balance the pencil across the top of the glass (photo B). This will keep the wick straight during the pouring and cooling stages.

3 Place the solid wax into the glass measuring cup, and set the measuring cup into the pan (photo C). Fill the pan with water about halfway up the measuring cup (creating a homemade double boiler). Set the stovetop burner on medium heat under the pan.

BUYING WAX

Conventional wax can be used in this project, but soy wax has lots of benefits over other waxes. Soy wax is non-toxic and burns cleaner than traditional wax. It also burns more slowly and lasts longer! Soy candles are a great gift for people with allergies or asthma, who may react to the smoke and soot produced by the petroleum in regular wax candles.

4 Place the thermometer into the wax, and watch the temperature carefully. Stir the wax as needed as it melts, and heat it to 160 degrees. Wax is flammable; for safety never heat wax above 165 degrees.

5 Wearing oven mitts, remove the measuring cup from the water and place it on a heat-proof surface. Leave the thermometer in the wax. When the wax temperature drops to 125 degrees, add fragrance oil (photo D) and stir thoroughly. For a tea glass that holds 2 cups of wax, use 20-40 drops of fragrance to scent the wax. Add more drops for a stronger scent.

6 Continue to watch the temperature of the wax. When it reaches 110 degrees, very slowly pour it into the glass. Fill to just below the rim. Make sure the wick is centered in the candle and taut.

7 Let your candles rest undisturbed at room temperature to harden. They may crack if disturbed while cooling, or if the area is too cool or drafty. When the wax is completely cooled, trim the wick to ¼ inch above the candle (photo E). Wait 4 days before lighting the candle in order to allow the fragrance to disperse throughout the wax.

TIPS | DIY Network Crafts

NUKE IT!

Soy wax can also be melted in the microwave. Just check the package for instructions.

CHOOSING FRAGRANCES

For Moroccan tea glasses, you may want to keep to the theme and choose rich, fruity aromatic scents like Bergamot, Fig, Red Currant, or Mandarin.

Have a small container of coffee beans at hand when working with fragrances. Taking a whiff of the coffee periodically between smelling fragrances will help you distinguish between them.

A little essential oil goes a long way but don't worry, it also keeps a long time. Use your oil in soap making, like the next project, or in other bath gifts.

SPICY TEA SOAPS

Pamper a friend with artistic gift soaps that you wrap yourself.

◣ **PROJECT SUMMARY** ◢

Blend your own mix of fragrant dried flowers and tea into glycerin soap for beautiful gift soaps. Then wrap them with bits of decorative paper and scrap ribbon for giving.

You Will Need

Glycerin soap base	Essential oil
Large kitchen knife	Colorant (optional)
Cutting block	Soap molds
Large glass measuring cup	Rubbing alcohol in spray bottle
Medium-sized pan and water	Decorative paper scraps
Stovetop	Ribbon scraps
Stirring spoon	Tape
Dried chamomile flowers	Tissue paper or cellophane
Dried lavender flowers	Glue stick
Herbal tea bags	Rubber stamps or stickers

1 Use a kitchen knife to cut the block of glycerin soap into 1-inch cubes (photo A). Place the cubes into the glass measuring cup. Set the measuring cup into the pan, and fill the pan with water to reach halfway up the outside of the measuring cup (photo B), creating a double boiler. Set the stovetop burner on medium heat under the pan.

2 Keep a watchful eye as the glycerin cubes melt—about 10 minutes. Stir as needed (photo C). Remove from heat and skim off any skin that forms on the surface of the glycerin.

TIPS | DIY Network Crafts

BUYING GLYCERIN SOAP
Glycerin soap base is sold in one-pound blocks or bags. It is readily available at most craft stores or from Internet-based soap-making suppliers.

3 Add the lavender, chamomile, and contents of the tea bags to the melted soap. Stir to combine (photo D). Add a few drops of essential oil, and colorant if desired, and mix well.

4 Pour the melted soap into the soap molds (photo E). If bubbles appear on the surface, use a spray bottle of rubbing alcohol to spritz the surface of the soap Allow the soap to harden and cool. Then, pop the soaps out of the molds.

5 To decorate rectangular soaps, recycle gift wrap by cutting strips to wrap around the bar. Secure the back with a small piece of tape, and tie off with a ribbon for extra pop. For round soaps, wrap tissue paper or cellophane around the soap, bringing the ends of the paper to the top of the bar. Seal it with a round piece of paper secured with glue. Decorate the paper with rubber stamps or stickers (photo F).

TIPS | DIY Network Crafts

MINTY FRESH

Herbal teas such as chamomile or mint make great additives to soap. Essential oils such as peppermint or grapefruit are a fresh and invigorating choice to go with them, or use lavender for a calming scent.

GLASS WINE STOPPER

Refashion an old glass drawer pull into a classy wine stopper. Try making a set to take with wine as a host or hostess gift for a party.

◢ **PROJECT SUMMARY** ◣

Drill through the center of a cork to attach it to a glass drawer pull with a cap screw. Cap screws can be found in various lengths at a local hardware store

You Will Need

Bottle-sized cork	Cap screw
Drill	Screwdriver
Glass drawer pull	

1 Mark the center of the cork, and drill a hole all the way through it (photo A).

2 Separate the cap screw into two parts (photo B). Working on the top of the cork, thread the screw portion through the glass knob and the cork (photo C).

3 Bring the cap portion of the screw through the bottom of the cork until it meets with the screw (photo D). Use a screwdriver to secure the cap and screw together.

A

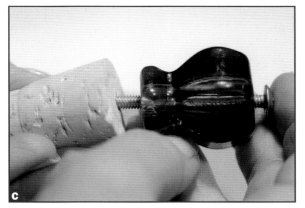

C

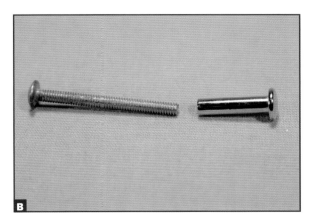

B

D

4

Play

Crafting is fun at every age. You don't have to be an experienced crafter to be creative. This chapter explores the fun you can have with the whole family—everything from a doll's bed to fabulous fairy wings. Grab the kids, and recycle those everyday items into creations that will send their imaginations running wild.

Cathie   Steve

BATH-TIME PUPPETS

Bath time is a whole lot more fun with a washcloth buddy customized to your child's favorite animal.

▆ **PROJECT SUMMARY** ▆

Sew a hand towel into a puppet in this project and embellish it with felt and embroidery stitches to create a fun bath-time piglet. You will need a sewing machine for this project.

You Will Need	
Hand towel	Sewing machine
Permanent marker	Felt scraps
Scissors	Embroidery floss
Straight pins	Embroidery needle

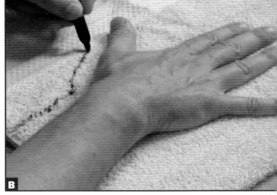

1 Fold the hand towel in half, end to end (photo A). Lay your hand on the folded towel with your arm toward an open edge of the towel. Spread your pinky and thumb as far as you can and, with a wide stroke (about 1½ inches from your hand), trace around your hand with the marker. Keep a wide opening at the base so you can insert your hand into the puppet (photo B).

2 Cut through both layers of the towel outside of the marked line (photo C), and pin together for sewing.

3 Sew around the puppet with a ¼-inch seam allowance (photo D). Keep the bottom of the puppet open for your hand.

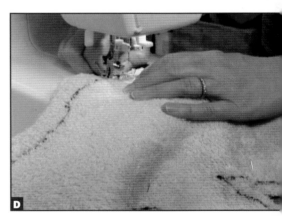

TIPS | DIY Network Crafts

BATH-TIME PETS
Make hand puppets into any animal you like: frogs, puppies, cats, silly monkeys— any animal you can think of. Just choose towel and felt colors appropriate for your animal and stitch away.

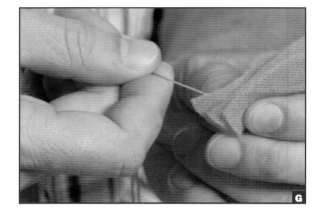

4 Make small notches in the seam allowance on the curved seams so when the material is turned, the edges are smoother (photo E). Turn the puppet right side out.

5 To add features to the puppet, be creative! Cut circles from felt to create the tummy, eyes, and nose. Stitch them into place by hand with embroidery floss, whipstitching around the outer edge (photo F).

6 To create the ears, cut a triangle shape from felt and pinch along the base of the triangle to create a gather. Make a few stitches to secure the gather at the bottom of the ear (photo G), then sew the ear in place on the puppet.

7 Use black embroidery floss to add extra details, like eyes and a nose, with a simple satin stitch (photo H). (For details on sewing a satin stitch, see page 60, Floral Button Cards.)

WHIPSTITCHING

Whipstitching is a basic hand-sewing stitch—an overhand stitch used to join two finished edges. The stitches cross the edge of the material, like hash marks, binding one material to the other. Insert the needle through the wrong side of the fabric, coming out onto the edge of one fabric. Make your first stitch into the other material, bringing the needle back up into the first fabric. Make another stitch into the second fabric, parallel to the first, the needle coming back up into the first fabric, resulting in stitches that are side-by-side rather than end to end.

A DOLL'S BED

Transform a simple bed tray into a doll's bed any little girl would love to make, complete with a comforter and furry bolster.

PROJECT SUMMARY

Use a wooden breakfast-in-bed tray and a foam cushion to fashion a little doll bed complete with flannel sheets, fleece bedspread, and a tiny fur bolster.

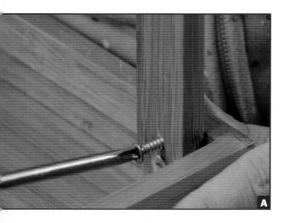

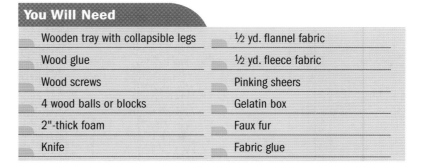

You Will Need

Wooden tray with collapsible legs	½ yd. flannel fabric
Wood glue	½ yd. fleece fabric
Wood screws	Pinking sheers
4 wood balls or blocks	Gelatin box
2"-thick foam	Faux fur
Knife	Fabric glue

1 Flip the bed tray over and use wood glue and screws to secure the legs in a locked-open position (photo A). The legs will be the head and footboard of the bed. Allow to dry.

2 Use the wood balls or blocks as legs for the bed, or drawer pulls will work as well. Attach them at the four corners with wood glue and allow to dry (photo B). Add long wood screws to secure them. Flip the bed over (photo C).

3 Cut the foam with a knife to fit the base of the tray (photo D)—this will be the mattress.

TIPS | DIY Network Crafts

PAINT IT
If you don't like the color of the tray, change it! Sand the tray, wipe off any dust, and paint it with acrylic paint.

4 Cut the flannel fabric to size for sheets to fit the foam mattress. Just tuck them into place, rather than gluing (photo E). Then they can be removed and washed later as they collect dust or dirt from little hands.

5 To make the comforter, cut a piece of fleece fabric slightly larger than the bed. Fleece is great for this use because it does not fray. Use pinking sheers on the edges of the comforter for a little pizzazz.

6 To make the fur bolster, open both ends of the gelatin box. Fold the flaps to the inside of the box. Cut a piece of faux fur that will wrap around the entire box with a little overhang on both ends.

7 Lay the fur wrong side up and place the box in the center. Wrap the fur around the box and secure with fabric glue (photo F). Tuck the edges of the fabric into the open box ends for a finished look (photo G).

E

F

G

CRAZY CRAYONS

Every kid has a bucket of old broken crayons that never see the light of day—until now! Recycle those crayon bits into funky Crazy Crayons in a few simple steps.

◣ **PROJECT SUMMARY** ◣

Melt unused crayons into new shapes using star candy molds, or any other shapes. Kids can be part of the fun helping to peel and break up the crayons.

You Will Need

Old broken crayons	Stovetop
Jars	Old pencils
Large saucepan	Oven mitt or hot pad
Water	Star-shaped candy molds

1 Sort the crayons by color family. (If you combine all of the colors, you will end up with all brown crayons.) Remove the paper from the crayons, and break each group into small pieces (photo A). Place each group of crayon bits into a separate jar.

2 Place the jars in the saucepan. Add water to the pan. The water level should be about halfway up the outside of the jars. This will serve as a double boiler to melt the crayons.

3 Place the pan on the stovetop over low or medium heat until the crayons are melted. Use old pencils to stir the crayons as they are melting (photo B).

4 When the wax is melted, use an oven mitt or hot pad to handle the jars, and pour the melted wax into the molds (photo C). Fill the mold with one color, or layer the colors by pouring a small amount of one color into the mold, allowing it to cool, adding the next color, allowing it to cool, and repeating until the mold is filled (photo D).

5 Allow the wax to cool and pop the crayons out of the molds. If they don t come out easily, place the mold in the freezer for about 20 minutes. Then they should pop right out.

TIPS | DIY Network Crafts

CREATIVE MOLDS
Use any kind of mold to make these fun crazy crayons: small cake tins, muffin pans, or even soap molds.

CRITTER HAT PUPPETS

For puppet shows and other playtime fun, this nest of crazy critters will spark kids' imaginations.

◣ **PROJECT SUMMARY** ◢

Craft this quick puppet toy from a garden glove and a straw hat using pom-poms for the critter heads. Glue on google eyes and assorted decorations to make the faces.

You Will Need

Scissors	Garden glove
Small straw hat	Google eyes
Double-fold bias tape	Assorted decorations
Hot glue and glue gun	Pipe cleaners
Assorted pom-poms	Eyelash yarn

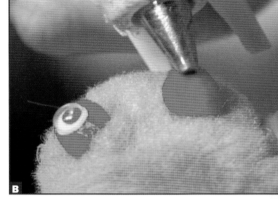

1 Use a scissors to cut a hole slightly larger than a wrist in the top of the hat.

2 Bind the cut edge by fitting double-fold bias tape over the edge and securing it with hot glue (photo A).

3 Glue a large pom-pom to each fingertip of the glove. Each pom-pom will be the head of one critter. Glue smaller pom-poms to the face, and add goggle eyes (photo B). Use your imagination to design facial features and add lots of fun details.

4 Bend pipe cleaners into zigzag shapes (photo C) and glue pom-poms to the ends to create funny ears and antennas.

5 Once the glove is complete with 5 critters, push it through the opening on the hat and secure it with a drop or two of hot glue (photo D)

6 Fill the inside of the hat around the glove with eyelash yarn as a nest for the critters.

TIPS | DIY Network Crafts

CHIRPERS

Instead of critters, you can easily create little chicks just by adding some small beaks made of felt to their faces.

SAFETY NOTE

Parents: If you are making these puppets for young children, avoid embellishments that could pose a choking hazard.

FAIRY WINGS

It doesn't have to be a special holiday for children to put on a costume and play make-believe in their own imaginary land. Kids will dance and delight in these easy-to-make wings.

Use wire hangers to frame the wings in this project and a few pairs of pantyhose as netting to cover them. Duct tape holds it all together, and elastic straps keep the wings in place on your little angel.

You Will Need

3 wire coat hangers
Duct tape
2 pairs colored pantyhose, size 3X
Needle and thread
Scissors
2 yd. elastic
2 large silk flowers
Decoration such as ribbon, glitter, fabric paint, feather trim, pearls, sequins, rhinestones

1 Bend one of the coat hangers into a loose oval shape to form one of the upper sections of the wings. Work with the curves already in the hanger, but reshape it so that the curves take the form of graceful butterfly wings. Secure the hook by bending it down into a loop. When you are satisfied with the shape, bend another hanger to match the first one for a matching set of top wings.

2 Shape the third hanger into the bottom of the wings by bending it up in the center, toward the hook, creating two lobes on the wing. Secure the hook by bending it down into a loop.

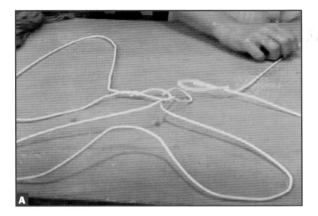

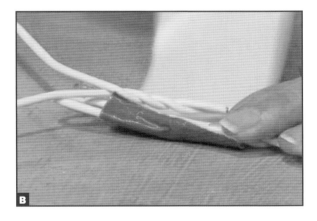

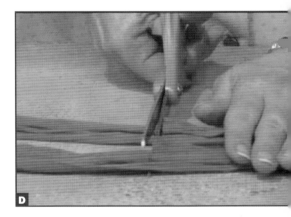

3 Lay the 3 hangers together with all hooks in the center. You will have two larger oval wings on the sides and a small bottom piece that slightly overlaps both wings. This should look like butterfly wings (photo A).

4 Using the duct tape, tape the hooks of the hangers together (photo B). Use as much tape as needed to fully cover the hooks and secure the frame (photo C).

5 Lay out one pair of pantyhose. Measure 20 inches up from each toe and cut (photo D). Stretch each leg over a bottom section of the wings. Pull tight and gather in the center of the wings (photo E). Loop, pull, and twist the excess hose around the center taped section. Using needle and thread, secure the hose with a whipstitch (see page 88).

6 Lay out the second pair of pantyhose. Measure 30 inches from each toe and cut. Working on the two upper sections of the wings, stretch each leg over an upper section. Pull tight and gather in the center. Loop, pull, and twist the excess hose around the center taped section. Using a needle and thread, secure this with a whipstitch as well.

7 To make two straps, cut the elastic into two 1-yard pieces. Fold each piece in half and wrap it underneath one upper side panel of the wings, and secure it with a knot. Repeat for the other side. Place the wings on your back and bring one elastic piece over your shoulder and the other piece under your arm. Tie a knot to secure. Repeat for the other side.

8 Glue the large flowers in the center of the wings to cover the duct tape and stitching. Embellish the wings with glitter, feather trim, ribbons, pearls, fabric paint, sequins, and rhinestones (photo F).

TIPS DIY Network Crafts

COLORFUL WINGS

Buy colored pantyhose for the wings in this project, or make wings in any color of the rainbow by tinting white pantyhose with fabric dye.

BUTTERFLY VARIATION

Use acrylic paints to make the wings look like a monarch butterfly (photo at right).

PAPER PRINCESS FLOWER

These fanciful fairy flowers are perfect for a little princess or as a crafty centerpiece.

PROJECT SUMMARY

Dip, dye, and snip coffee filters to create whimsical flowers on a chopstick stem.

You Will Need

Glass bowl

Water

Food coloring

5 to 10 basket-style coffee filters

Paper towels

Newspaper or waxed paper

Scissors

1 chopstick

Floral tape

1 Fill the bowl with water, and add food coloring for the dye bath. Add a stack of coffee filters to the bath (photo A).

A

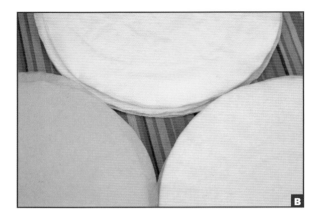

2 When the filters are the desired color, remove them from the dye bath, and squeeze out the excess dye. Place the wet filters on a paper towel with newspapers or waxed paper underneath, and allow the filters to dry (photo B).

3 To make the petals, use 5 to 10 filters per flower. Fold each filter in half and in half again to make a quarter pie shape (photo C). With scissors, cut curved or spiked shapes around the curved edge of the filter, cutting through all layers (photo D). Experiment with different shapes (photo E). Repeat this step for every filter.

TIPS | DIY Network Crafts

DYEING FOR COLOR

Use quite a bit of food coloring in the dye bath—the filters dry much lighter than they appear when wet. The longer you leave them in the bath, the darker the color. Remove them quickly for a lighter shade.

4 Open the cut filters. Poke the chopstick through the center of the first petal (photo F), gather the petal to the end of the chopstick, and twist the base of the petal around the chopstick. Secure with floral tape (photo G). Add more layers of petals and floral tape until the flower is full (photo H).

5 Wrap the entire chopstick with green floral tape to create the stem (photo I).

TIPS | DIY Network Crafts

USING FLORAL TAPE

Floral tape is available in green and brown colors. The tape becomes tacky when stretched. Cut off a length of tape, hold one end in each hand, stretch it, and it's ready to use.

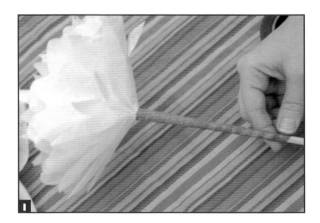

TRAVEL TIC-TAC-TOE

Kids will travel back in time with this classic tic-tac-toe game made modern with a metal CD case. Make one for the car and one for each child's backpack and you'll always have entertainment on the go.

PROJECT SUMMARY

Ribbons, buttons, and magnets are all it takes to turn a plain metal CD case into a tic-tac-toe game for endless fun. You'll need fray retardant for this project, available at most fabric stores.

You Will Need	
Metal CD case	Embroidery floss
Thin ribbon	Embroidery needle
Fray retardant	10 buttons, 4-hole
Metal embellishment glue	10 magnet discs
2 flat metal scrapbook letters "X"	Heavy-duty glue
2 flat metal scrapbook letters "O"	

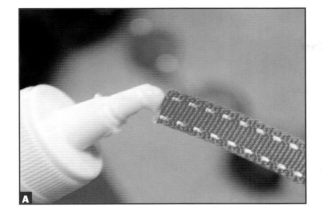

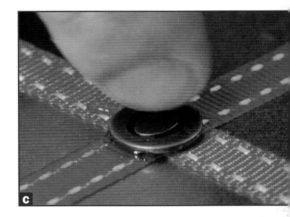

1 Remove the inside CD holders from the metal case. Game pieces will be stored inside the case when not in use. Trim two pieces of ribbon to fit across the width of the case and two pieces to fit the length of the case. Add a drop of fray retardant to the ends of the ribbon to keep them intact (photo A).

2 Use metal embellishment glue to attach the ribbons to the top of the case in a crisscross pattern, forming the tic-tac-toe board (photo B).

3 Use a drop of metal embellishment glue to secure the flat scrapbook letters where the ribbons cross (photo C).

4 To make the game pieces, use embroidery floss and stitch an X into 5 buttons through the 4 holes (photo D). Use the same technique to stitch an O into 5 buttons.

5 Use heavy-duty glue to adhere magnets to the backs of the buttons.

TIPS | DIY Network Crafts

COLOR ME FUN

Use two different colors of embroidery thread for the X buttons and O buttons for variety and to help set the game pieces apart.

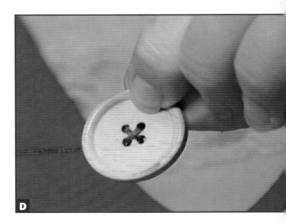

WILD PARTY HATS

Let the kids get their party on with these fun hats made from an old paper bag and lots of fun decorations.

◀ PROJECT SUMMARY ▶

Start with a paper bag, a little paint, and lots of decorations for this big party hat. Or, make a point with a cone hat crafted from scrapbook paper.

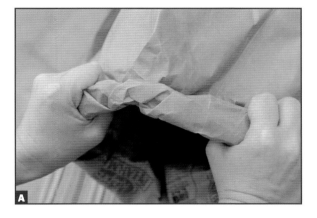

PAPER BAG HAT

You Will Need

Paper grocery bags	Glitter
Silver craft paint	White glue
Foam paintbrush	Pom-poms
Scissors	Pipe cleaners
Felt	Tacky glue or hot glue and glue gun
Styrofoam balls	

1 To build the hat brim, gently roll down the top of the bag until it reaches the desired size. Pinch the brim to adjust the fit as needed (photo A).

2 Paint the paper hat with silver craft paint and allow to dry (photo B).

3 Make tons of fun decorations: Cut star shapes out of felt. Make glittery styrofoam balls using white glue and glitter. Fashion antennas by coiling the ends of pipe cleaners and adding pom-poms on the ends (photo C).

4 Use hot glue or tacky glue to attach the decorations to the hat (photo D).

◣ CONE HAT ◢

You Will Need

12x12 scrapbook paper
Stapler
Scissors
Hot glue and glue gun
Large silk flower with stem
Eyelets
Eyelet setter
10-15" elastic cording
Decoration such as silk flowers, lady bugs, streamers, glitter, paint, rhinestones, stickers.

1 Roll the sheet of scrapbook paper into a cone shape, and staple the bottom edge to secure it (photo A).

2 Use scissors to trim away the excess paper to make a rounded bottom on the hat (photo B) and a smooth seam up the side of the hat (photo C).

3 Add a drop of hot glue to the inside of the seam if needed (photo D), and hot glue the flower's stem over the seam on the cone for decoration (photo E).

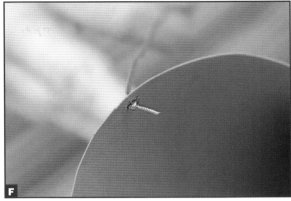

4 To make a chin strap, use the eyelet hole punch and setter to attach two eyelets to the hat one on each side at the base. Thread the elastic cording through one of the eyelets (photo F) and tie off. Tie the other end of the cord through the other eyelet.

5 Use hot glue to decorate the hat with silk flowers, plastic lady bugs, streamers, ribbons, glitter, paint, embellishments, or whatever fun idea you have (photo G). Go crazy here and really show your creativity.

5

Remember

Looking for a few decorating tips? Well, you don't have to look further than a stack of old books or a beautiful piece of paper. We turn the most ordinary items into spectacular pieces of art. Everyone knows recycling is good but who knew it could be so much fun! Check out some of the projects we created when we took a second look at the things you might otherwise have thrown out.

Cathie   Steve

MATCHBOX TREASURE CHEST

Tiny drawers made from matchboxes keep precious treasures safely tucked away. Buttons and beads make fancy drawer pulls for a decorative touch.

◧ **PROJECT SUMMARY** ◪

Using beads as drawer pulls, glue matchboxes into a tower to create this treasure chest, and dress it up with decorative paper and ribbon. The beads or pearls for this project must be small enough to fit on the front of the matchbox drawer.

You Will Need

5 small matchboxes	Tape measure
Craft paint	Decorative paper
Small paintbrush	Scissors
5 small beads or pearls	1 yd. ribbon
Heavy-duty glue	Charms, beads, or sparkles
Glue stick	

1 Remove the inside "drawer" section of each matchbox and paint the front, back, and side edges with craft paint and a small paintbrush (photo A).

2 Allow to dry. Using heavy-duty glue, adhere a bead or pearl to the center of each drawer front to form a small knob.

3 Use a glue stick to glue the boxes together in a stack.

4 Then, measure around the stack of matchboxes (photo B) and add ¼ inch to that measurement for the length of the paper in the next step. Measure the depth of the stack, from back to front. This is the width for the paper in the next step.

5 Using the measurements determined in the previous step, cut a strip of decorative paper to size. Glue the decorative paper around the stack of matchboxes (photo C).

6 Wrap the entire stack with ribbon, and tie a decorative bow at the top (photo D). Embellish the treasure chest with additional charms, beads, and other sparkles, if desired.

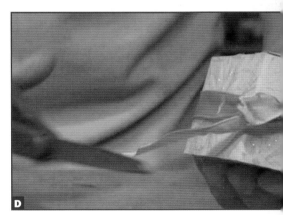

TIPS | DIY Network Crafts

SUPER TREASURE CHEST

Matchboxes too small for your treasures? Take it up a notch by using the larger boxes from wooden kitchen matches instead!

FABRIC-COVERED SCRAPBOOK

Transform an outdated photo album into a boutique-worthy scrapbook using your favorite fabric design and ribbon.

PROJECT SUMMARY

Use fabric and batting to revive an old photo album or three-ring notebook. Measure the book cover dimensions to determine the length of quilter's batting needed.

You Will Need

Thin quilter's batting	Hot glue and glue gun
Outdated photo album	Thin cardboard
Tacky glue	Ruler
Scissors	Fusible webbing
2½-yard pieces of decorative fabrics	Silk flowers, ribbons, scrapbook embellishments (optional)
Iron	

1 Glue the batting to the front of the photo album using tacky glue (photo A). Trim around the edges of the book to remove any excess batting.

2 Press the fabric with an iron. Lay the fabric wrong side up and position the opened book, batting side down, on top of the fabric (photo B). Trim the fabric, keeping a 2-inch border around the book to allow enough to wrap it.

3 Apply a bead of hot glue to the inside corner edge of the notebook, and fold the material over the corner. Repeat for each corner (photo C).

4 Apply a bead of glue around each edge of the book (photo D), and fold the material snugly over the edge onto the glue. Try closing the book as you work to be sure to allow enough fabric to cover the spine.

5 Make two cuts in the fabric border at the top of the spine and the bottom of the spine. Trim the resulting flap of fabric at the spine, if needed, to allow for the three-ring closer or other binding (photo E). Add a bead of hot glue, and secure the fabric over the spine edges as well.

6 Measure the inside covers of the notebook as close to the edge as possible. Cut the cardboard to that measurement. Cut two pieces of iron-on, fusible webbing and two pieces of the inside decorative fabric at least 1 inch larger than the cardboard on all sides.

7 Layer the inside decorative fabric, fusible webbing, and cardboard together. Attach the fabric to the cardboard using a hot iron. First, press the topside of the fabric to the cardboard (photo F), then turn the cardboard over and press the edges of the fabric over the edges of the cardboard.

8 Use hot glue to attach the fabric-covered cardboard to the inside cover of the book (photo G).

9 Use hot glue to add additional details and embellishments to the front cover of the book. Silk flowers, name plaques, ribbons—the sky is the limit!

TIPS | DIY Network Crafts

SCRAPBOOK LIKE A PRO

Many stores are devoted entirely to scrapbooking. They often supply new and creative ways to improve your scrapbook pages. Try visiting scrapbooking stores to find out how to transform your scrapbooks from mere picture albums to cherished mementos.

WORD GAME FUNKY FRAME

These funky decorated frames will spell fun on any wall or shelf. Display one alone or make several for a matching set.

◣ **PROJECT SUMMARY** ◥

Revamp a blank picture frame with decorative paper and use word game letter tiles and trays to create a personal message.

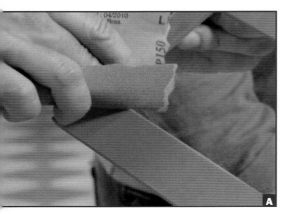

You Will Need

Wood frame with a large face	Scissors
Craft paint	Paper glue
Foam paintbrush	Word game letter tray
Fine grit sandpaper	Word game letter tiles
Scrapbook paper, 2 colors	Heavy-duty glue
Pencil	Ribbon trim

1 Paint the frame using the foam brush and craft paint. Allow to dry. Lightly sand the edges of the frame to wear away some of the paint (photo A).

2 Trace the frame onto the backside of a piece of scrapbook paper, going around the outside edge of the frame and the inside edge of the opening. Cut slightly inside of the traced lines, to create a smaller paper front (photo B).

3 Cut small strips of paper as wide as you choose to fit around the scrapbook paper as a border. Use a contrasting color for added detail.

4 Use paper glue to attach the cut scrapbook paper to the front of the frame (photo C).

5 Next, attach the paper border using the same paper glue (photo D). Press out any air bubbles with your fingers.

6 Use craft paint to paint the letter tray in a complementary or matching color. Allow to dry.

7 Choose letters to spell out a word, such as "GROW" to complement a photo of kids playing in a tree. Line up the letters on the tray (photo E).

8 Attach the letters to the tray by dotting the backs of the letter tiles with heavy-duty glue (photo F) and placing them on the tray. Allow to dry.

9 Glue the letter tray to the frame using heavy-duty glue. Position the tray on the frame in any way you like, setting it level across the bottom, off to the side, or even a bit crooked for interest. Finish it off with ribbon.

E

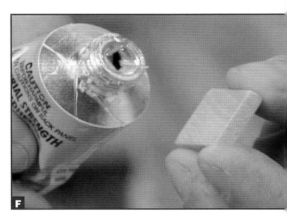

F

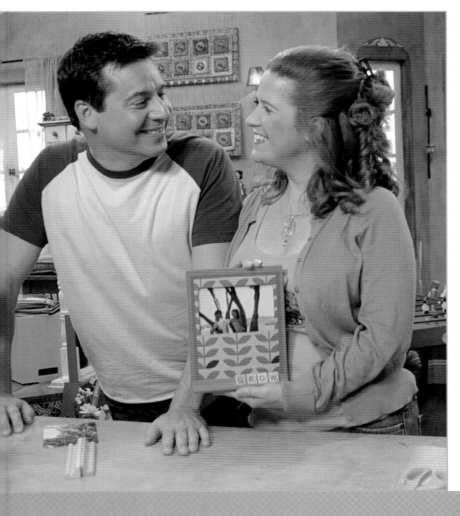

TIPS | DIY Network Crafts

FUN AND GAMES

Don't have an old word game? Check local thrift shops for used games and bags of mismatched pieces.

FAMILY HEIRLOOM BROOCH

Create a vintage-style, family heirloom brooch with a small family photo and old eyeglasses.

 PROJECT SUMMARY

Use a lens from an old pair of glasses to hold a family image, then use decoupage medium to give it dimension and sheen. Make sure the glasses you choose for this project are not bifocals! The decoupage medium will work better with color laser copies than with real photos, and you can size the photo just right with a copier.

You Will Need

Old pair of eyeglasses	Craft paint
Color-copied photo	Decorative trim
Decorative scrap paper	Tacky glue
Scissors	Pin back
Decoupage medium	Heavy-duty glue
Small paintbrush	

1 Remove the glass lenses from the eyeglass frames.

2 Use a piece of decorative scrap paper as a backdrop for the photo, trimming it to fit inside the glass lens. Then, trim the photo to fit on the paper as desired (photo A).

A

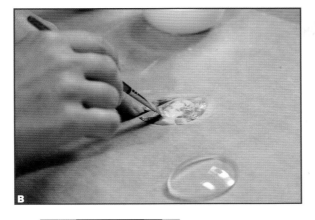

TIPS | DIY Network
Crafts

FINDING GLASSES

If you don't have a pair of old eyeglasses to use, you can pick up gobs of them at a local thrift shop for only a few bucks!

3 Apply decoupage medium to the front and back of the photo and the scrap paper. Layer them in place (photo B).

4 Press the decoupaged photo and scrap paper into the eyeglass lens with the photo toward the glass. With your finger, press out any air bubbles (photo C). Allow to dry. The decoupage medium will dry clear.

5 Apply a coat of craft paint to the back of the image and glass (photo D). Allow to dry. Apply several coats, allowing each to dry before applying the next. The paint will appear opaque.

6 Cut decorative trim to fit around the edge of the glass. Using tacky glue, adhere the trim to the edge. Use heavy-duty glue to attach the pin back, and allow to dry (photo E).

MOSAIC BUTTON FRAME

Button button whose got the button? You do with this fancy recycled button frame. All you need now is a photo.

◀ **PROJECT SUMMARY** ▶

Use buttons and grout in this project to remake an old frame. Be sure to use rubber gloves with the messy grout. This technique can be used on a frame, small clay pot, or tea tray.

You Will Need

Old buttons	Rubber gloves
Heavy-duty glue	Plastic spatula
Bamboo skewer or toothpick	Sponge or paper towel
Blank frame	Small bucket of water
Ultra-fine grout	Craft paint
	Paintbrush

1 Apply heavy-duty glue to the backs of the buttons, using a toothpick, if needed (photo A). Glue the buttons to the front of the frame in a random pattern, and allow to dry.

2 Mix the grout according to the manufacturer's instructions. Wearing rubber gloves and using a plastic spatula, spread the grout over the buttons and frame. Work the grout in between the buttons, and let it set (photo B).

3 Once set, use a damp sponge or paper towel to wipe away the excess grout until the tops of the buttons are clear of grout (photo C). Rinse the sponge as needed in water. Allow the frame to dry.

4 Apply craft paint to the edges of the frame with a paintbrush (photo D), and allow to dry.

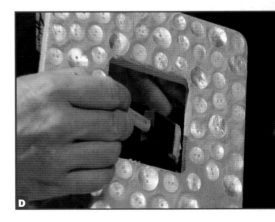

TIPS | DIY Network
Crafts

NEED BUTTONS?

Check your clothes for extra buttons; most garments come with spares. Or, find tons of mismatched buttons at thrift or vintage stores.

SHIPPING TAG SCRAPBOOK

Shipping tags are easily transformed into tiny scrapbooks filled with cherished memories.

◀ **PROJECT SUMMARY** ▶

Decorate shipping tags with family photos and clippings of memorabilia for this fun, mini scrapbook. One long ribbon provides the hinges for the pages. Find shipping tags in various sizes and colors at most office supply stores.

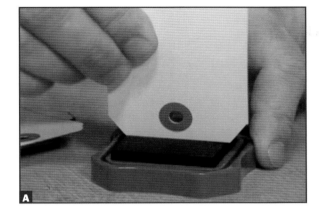

You Will Need

P12 large shipping tags	Scissors
Pigment ink pad	Scrapbook embellishments
1 yd. grosgrain ribbon	Rubber stamps
Heavy-duty, acid-free paper glue	Fun scrap papers
	Decorative ribbons and yarns
Photos of family and friends	

1 Rub the edges of the shipping tags along the ink pad to create an antiqued edge (photo A). Allow to dry.

2 Lay out five of the tags on your work surface, side by side, about ½ inch apart.

3 Glue the strip of grosgrain ribbon across the center of all 5 tags using a heavy-duty glue (photo B). Don't place glue on the ribbon in between the tags.

4 Glue the remaining five tags on top of the five tags with the ribbon. You will decorate both sides of the tags.

5 Add fun scrapbooking embellishments, stickers, and family photos to create a cover for the booklet on the first tag. Decorate each additional tag with photos and memorabilia until all the tags are covered on both sides (photo C).

6 Thread ribbons and yarn scraps through the holes on the tags to create texture and interest (photo D). Then, fold up the tags into a mini scrapbook!

RECYCLED GIFT CRAFTS

Cherished memories are often saved in greeting cards and notes, and now with a few simple techniques you can create a few fun memory projects for your home.

◣ PROJECT SUMMARY ◢

Use greeting card cutouts and a little glue to form these colorful, round ornament balls, or make garland, gift tags, and candle wraps.

You Will Need

Used greeting cards	Bone folder or ruler
2½" punch	Paper glue
Pencil	Clothespins
Scissors	⅛" hole punch
Cardboard scrap	Decorative ribbon

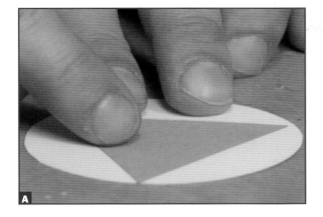

ORNAMENT BALL

1 Use the 2½-inch punch to punch 20 circles from assorted cards.

2 Cut out a triangle of cardboard that measures 2⅛ inches on all sides to use as a template. Trace the triangle onto the back of each greeting card circle (photo A).

3 Score each circle along the triangle lines using the bone folder or ruler. Fold the circle so that the printed sides of each circle are on the interior of a small, triangle-shaped bowl (photo B).

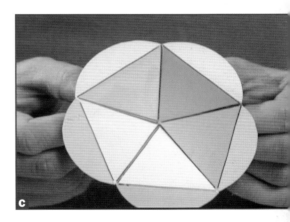

4 Using five of the scored circles, glue the flap of one circle to the flap of another, continuing with all five circles to form a star shape (photo C). If needed, use clothespins to clamp the edges together until they dry—about 15 minutes.

5 Working with 10 more greeting card circles, create the middle layer, gluing these flaps to the bottom layer flaps (photo D). Allow to dry.

6 Use the last five greeting card circles to form the top layer. Glue the same way and allow to dry.

7 Punch one section of a glued flap with the ⅛-inch hole punch, thread with a length of decorative ribbon, and hang.

GARLAND, GIFT TAGS, & CANDLE WRAPS

Cut out festive shapes from greeting cards using decorative paper punches. Use the paper shapes to string your own garland, create gift tags, decorate candles—or all three.

You Will Need

Several used greeting or note cards

Various large decorative paper punches

⅛" hole punch

Eyelets

Eyelet setter

Craft hammer

Decorative ribbon

1 Use various sizes and shapes of paper punches to make cutouts from greeting cards.

2 Use the ⅛-inch hole punch to punch holes at the top of each cutout for garland, or on the sides for candle wraps, or at the center top for gift tags.

3 Put an eyelet through a punched hole and use the eyelet setter and craft hammer to secure it. Repeat for all punched holes.

4 For garland, thread the greeting card shapes onto ribbon, spacing the shapes evenly apart.

5 For gift tags, thread each tag onto a length of ribbon, knot, and tie to packages.

6 For candle wraps, thread ribbon through the eyelets, wrap around a candle, and tie a bow.

◢ GREETING CARD SACHETS ◣

Using scissors, a hole punch, and potpourri and tulle fabric inside a favorite greeting card, you'll be able create a unique sachet for hanging for gift giving.

1 Use the scissors to trim a greeting card to a smaller size, if desired. Be sure to not trim the folded edge.

2 Use the hole punch to make several holes in the front and back of the card. These are the airholes for the sachet fragrance to waft through.

3 Trim two pieces of tulle slightly smaller than each side of the card, then glue both to the inside of the card with a glue stick, one on the inside front, one on the inside back.

4 Pour a small mound of potpourri, dried lavender, or a couple of cinnamon sticks onto the center of the tulle inside the card.

5 Cut a 12-inch length of decorative ribbon, form it into a loop, and tuck the ends inside the top of the card. This will be the loop to hang the sachet.

6 Line the inside edges of one side of the card with hot glue.

7 Fold the sides together and press to bond. Be sure that the ribbon loop is well secured. Allow the glue to cool, and hang the sachet.

ACKNOWLEDGMENTS

A big thank you to all our family and friends. Without their support and love we would have no *Creative Juice*. Special thanks to Jennifer Garcia Manley (pages 31, 47, 54, 92, 96, 98, and 110), Jack Parker (front cover), and Zuzanna Pakula vel Rutka (all other images) for their fabulous photos and tireless energy. A huge hug and thanks to Jennifer Merrick, Gina Zycher, Elizabeth West, and Ann Nord for all the love they bring to the projects, to Spencer "Beach Buddha" for pulling all the step-by-step pics, to Sierra Angel for her "Rockabilly" artwork on the denim cuffs. Thanks to Greg Byers, our producing partner, for going on this creative journey and to the entire *Creative Juice* crew and everyone at DIY Network and Lark Books. And last, but not least, to Eddie Filian (Cathie's Hubby) for putting up with all the glitter and glue.